Tribal India: Issues and Challenges

Tracker (Snatan) on the Chanshal Peak

Tribal India

Issues and Challenges

Mridula Sharda
Inder Kumar

Rawat Publications
Jaipur • New Delhi • Bangalore • Guwahati • Kolkata

ISBN 978-81-316-1200-2

Published by

Prem Rawat for **Rawat Publications**
Satyam Apts., Sector 3, Jawahar Nagar, Jaipur 302 004 (India)
Phones: 0141 265 1748 / 265 7006
E-mail: info@rawatbooks.com
Website: www.rawatbooks.com

New Delhi Office
4858/24, Ansari Road, Daryaganj, New Delhi 110 002
Phone: 011-23263290

Also at *Bangalore, Guwahati* and *Kolkata*

Typeset by Rawat Computers, Jaipur

Printed and bound in India

Dedicated to
Hima, Shallu, Sanatan and Kovid, our loved ones

Contents

Foreword

India is a country of diverse communities. Tribal are known as Adivasis or *aborigines* which means first or original dwellers of a land, or aborigines. They are one of the most important segments of the Indian society. The tribal population of India is 8.9 per cent of the total population of the country. It is 20 per cent of the world's tribal population. The tribal society of India is heterogeneous. Location and geographical conditions are the determining factor of their socio-economic and political character. Despite their heterogeneity there are some common characteristics among them. They have common problems since centuries and in the present times also they face similar challenges. Special provisions of reservation and right to protect their cultural identity (Article 29–30) have been made in the Indian Constitution. To bring them in the mainstream, provisions in the Directive Principles of Indian Constitution have been included. The Constitution makers were well aware about the problems and concerns of these vulnerable sections of the society.

Since independence, successive governments have made efforts to develop the tribes of India. After more than seventy years of the independence, these endeavours yield mixed results. Nevertheless, tribes need special rational policy framework to meet their problems. Tribal people reside in the remote areas of the country. Either they live in the forests or near the forests. Mostly the terrain is hard and it is a tough task to develop infrastructure in these areas. Poor connectivity, lack of educational institutions and limited health care facilities are the main causes of their vulnerability. In addition to these hassles outer world's disability to understand their concerns and to involve them in the political economic process has made the situation worse.

Panchayats Extension to the Scheduled Areas 1996 (PESA Act 1996) on the lines of the Seventy-Third Amendment of the Indian

Constitution could be considered as a landmark step in the history of tribal empowerment. The Act provides community power to the tribal people, determine the development contours and be a part of the grassroots democracy. Empowered Gram Sabha would be an institution to keep check on the activities of the outsiders as well as act as the nursery of democratic set up of the Indian system.

The New Economic Policy (NEP) of 1991 opened the doors of the tribal world to the corporate sector. The corporates have been given liberty to conduct economic activities in the remote areas which are rich in natural resources, especially water resources. But flexibility and changed economic scenario disturbed the tribal society at large. Tribal life style, their age-old social, religious and economic system has been challenged by the influx of the outsiders. Physical ecology has also been disturbed by the excessive use of natural resources. This attempts to provide ample information regarding the tribal ethnography. It deals with the Constitutional provisions and has evaluated the given provisions in the contemporary situation.

In the last twenty-five years (1995–2020) two developments of the Indian system, i.e. NEP and Democratic Decentralisation (PESA Act 1996), brought a paradigm shift in the tribal life. The author have critically analysed both the processes and highlighted their impact on the tribes. Liberalisation, Globalisation and Privatisation posed challenges to the tribal identity. To protect and promote the culture and diversity within the Constitution was the first and foremost mission of our national leaders at the time of freedom. This book deals extensively with the issues on these lines. By analysing the empowerment issues within the gambit of the PESA Act, a thorough study has been undertaken to evaluate the empowerment of all sections in the tribal society. We have to understand the concept of people's participation as a pre-requisite for the democracy and development of the tribal society. Experiences of the tribal people have been analysed and illustrated – these have immense importance for the future policy formulation and planning.

This book is of great use for the academicians, policy makers, tribes and is of interest to all within and outside the tribal communities who are really sensitive to the needs of the tribes.

Dr Ram Lal Markanda
Technical Education, T.D.
I.T. & RPG Minister, Himachal Pradesh

Prelude

The real spirit of democracy lies in participation of the people in the political processes and political development at the different levels. Keen interest in the politics should come up as an instinct and the public must regularly follow political developments. They must be aware about the public policies and the development programmes initiated by the state. Their active participation in the political processes through different institutions in an organised manner is the only way out to evolve a stable democratic society.

Participatory democracy stands for the 'governance through popular authorisation'. Abraham Lincoln's popular statement 'government of the people by the people and for the people', meant the participation of the masses in the political arena. In the Indian context democracy means participation of the masses in the political processes to determine their goals and active participation at the implementation and evaluation of those programmes. At the grassroots level constitutional arrangements were made by the Seventy Third Amendment to convert the elite democracy in the participatory democracy through the system of Panchayati Raj Institutions (PRIs) in rural areas. Rural masses of India constitute 70 per cent of the total population of the country within the rural population 8.6 per cent population of the countries is the tribal population. Tribal segment of the Indian population is one of the important segments of the country's demography. Tribals have their distinct features. They are cultural identities living in the remote areas of the country. They are habitants of the different parts of the country. Indian tribal society is heterogeneous. Within the tribes there are sub-groups, sub groups have their own socio-economic and political life which differs from one to other according to the local ecology. Besides their multiple diversities they have some common characteristics and issues such as poverty, socio-economic backwardness and challenges to their society from the corporate are common to all. Those issues can be addressed on the pan India level. Tribes are the third most vulnerable section of the Indian society after the Scheduled Castes and women. On the development scale they are far behind the mainstream society. It is important to understand the 'Tribal Situation in India' to bring them at par with the mainstream society. It was the main goal of the constitution maker to bring the diverse sections of the Indian society on such a platform where everybody should find oneself in dignified position. Society should be based on the principle of liberty, equality and social justice to realise the dream of our leaders. PESA Act 1996 is a benchmark initiative on the lines of the Seventy Third Amendment of the Indian Constitution. PESA Act was introduced to meet the needs of the tribals in the V Schedule of the Constitution of India. Tribals have not been able to reach the approprite scale of development after independence.

Present work is devoted to understand the tribals, their ethnographic situation and the steps taken by the different levels of the government to improve their situation. In this field constitutional developments and the various articles concerning the tribals have been described and analysed in the present situation in the first part of the book.

Sub tribal groups in the states where the tribal population rate is quite high has been narrated in the book. Bihar, Odhisa, Madhya Pradesh are the three main states those have large chunk of the tribal population. Himachal Pradesh (HP) is a hilly state having three tribal pockets, has its own distinct tribal identity. On the basis of the development scale all three pockets are the developed tribes in comparison to the other tribals of the country. Detailed study of the HP tribes is one of the major components of the work. One chapter is devoted to each tribe of the state.

It is important to understand the tribal situation after the enactment of the PESA Act 1996 and the liberalisation of the Indian economy. PESA empowered the tribals to have effective voice in deciding their fate and managing their resources. Liberalisation provided the space to the corporate to intervene in the tribal areas for the development purposes. It is imperative to understand the functioning of the two processes as to understand how far both are able to do justice with the constitutional goals concerning the marginalised in the society. Do the tribes compete to protect their interests from the outside world when the scheduled areas are opened for the corporate activities? Is the corporate world interested to deal with these tribal identities according to their wishes? Last part of the book is devoted to these issues. In this part question of the tribal communities in relation to the corporate has been addressed. Empirical study is conducted in the tribal areas of Himachal Pradesh where hydro-power projects in the tribal areas have become common phenomenon. In the last two decades tribals are experiencing corporate pressures. Corporate activities in the tribal areas have posed challenge to the tribals who have little knowledge about these activities. These activities maligned the tribal societies and affected the natural ecology and disturbed their economic patterns. Being a native of Himachal and having special interest in the tribal community I felt the need to understand the complex problems of the tribals in the changing conditions. With the help of my student Inder Kumar, we both tried reach the root of the problems. Last part of the book is focused on the diverse dimensions of the Indian tribes in the twenty first century through the tribal experiences of Himachal Tribes.

It is the first and foremost duty to recognise the precious efforts of all those who have directly or indirectly contributed to accomplish this work. I extent my thanks to the tribal community of the Himachal, which provided me information without any hesitation. I am thankful to the academicians who always given me generous encouragement, assisted me and provided direction to my work. Professor Anand Kumar, Professor M.P. Singh and Professor H.S. Parmar's suggestions proved to be great help in developing the theoretical framework for the work. Without adequate academic resources it was not possible to take up this project. I am thankful to the IIAS library staff, who always welcomed me in the library and facilitated my library visits. I am thankful to my brother Ravi Chaudhary who edited this work. My special thanks to my family, friends and students, particularly the male members of my family who really played important role in every academic project of mine. I am thankful to my loving kids Mithu, Sanatan and Pawan. I am thankful to my loving relatives, my parents, father-in-law Kukkoo bhai, Ashwani bhai and younger ones Manu and Nidhi who left us behind in this worldly journey. I have no words to express my gratitude to my revered brother Professor N.K. Sharda who inspired me from childhood till date. Ajay my husband deserves heartfelt thanks who always kept patience to wear my constant academic involvement.

Mridula Sharda

1

Introduction

Democracy stands for direct or indirect role of the people in the governance. This term has been derived from two Greek words – demos (meaning people) and Kratia (rule). Abraham Lincoln once described it as 'the government of the people, for the people and by the people'. In the olden times, particularly during the days of the ancient city-states of Greece, when the size of the state was small and a huge chunk of its population (comprising women, children and slaves) had not been granted the status of citizens, people directly governed themselves (Bhatnagar 1984: 250). Democracy has, with the changing times, evolved in accordance with the prevailing conditions of the societies but its basic component ultimate power to govern is the right of the masses is same. Democracy means the power of the people. In a democratic form of the government, the ultimate power must be vested with the people. If the people do not have the ultimate power, in spite of the apparent political form, it cannot be called a democratic government (Das 1999: 171). In a democracy, it is assumed that there will be a diversity of opinions and interests on almost every matter of the main concern. Indeed, this diversity is seen as its main strength and it calls for tolerance towards all shades of the opinion. A democratic society is also called an 'open society' where there is space for all voices, however unpopular or conventional they may be (Srinivasan 2008: 109). There is a very close relationship between democracy and political participation. Democracy and political participation go together. For the efficient and successful working of the government, people's active participation is imperative. People's participation in their political system mainly depends upon their political attitude, values and beliefs (Mehta 2005: 271). Participation is an effective measure to give concrete shape to the political democracy. Process of the participation depends on the institutions, political structures and roles in the society. In a country where people have direct or indirect involvement in the political process from the local level to the national level, democracy is bound to be more effective as compared to the societies where people have only voting rights and they do not have involvement in planning, implementation and evaluation of the political decisions of the state. In case of India, where the supreme law of the country (Constitution) advocates the democracy as the basic feature of the Indian political system, it is important to understand its connotation in this context. Democracy implies all the sections of the Indian society despite their inequalities should enjoy equal right to be effective part of the Indian political system. After the Independence, electoral process from the local elections to the national elections is an evidence of the progressive democratic development. Rising voter turnout, involvement of all the sections in the political processes and peaceful change of the government through constitutional measures are the features those helped the country to be designated as successful political democracy. On the other side, increasing inequalities, economic status of the representatives from panchayat to the Lok Sabha forces one to think the factual status of the Indian democracy.

Participation

True citizenship involves meaningful participation in politics. To be meaningful for citizens, participation must at a minimum level be voluntary and consequential. Although political participation might appear rather straightforward, a close look reveals some ironies in the participatory process. It is sometimes deceptive also. In totalitarian systems, participation is sometimes most extensive, whereas it is sometimes meaningless because the state commands everybody to participate in the electoral process. It is not willful participation. By contrast, political participation is hit-or-miss in democratic countries, where citizens are free to decide whether to participate or not.

The word 'participation' refers to those voluntary activities by which the members of a society take part in the decision-making in the different processes and aspects of the development activities at the different levels of the government. It implies that people do so as matter of their role as sovereign in the democratic form of the government. The area of their participation involves administrative decisions and implementation of the development activities. The real purpose of the participation is to develop the human capabilities for the decision-making skills. Participation means a kind of the local autonomy in which people discover the possibilities of exercising their choice and thereby becoming capable of managing their own development.

Participation as defined in a UNESCO document is 'collective sustained activity for the purpose of achieving some common objectives, especially a more equitable distribution of the benefits of the development'. Although participation is defined in different ways, the dominant view is to regard it as a strategy to improve the development process (UNESCO 1978: 15). Cohen and Uphoof defined participation as 'people's participation in the decision-making' (Cohen and Uphoof 1980: 213). Santhanam's definition gives wider meaning to the term. According to him participation as commitment on the part of the individual towards all forms of action by which the individual can 'take part' or 'play role' in the operation without being conscious of the socio-economic barriers, to achieve certain common goals in a group situation. Jadav (1985: 68) emphasises on the voluntary participation of the people. In his perspective 'involvement of the people in the development process voluntarily and willingly, such participation cannot be coerced'. The synthesis of the given views of the scholars is participation involves mass involvement in the activities and deciding the goals, those are of the common interest. There are plenty of words analogous to the term participation, viz. involvement, support, empowerment, mobilisation, joining-in, co-operation, etc. (Joseph 1997: 53–54).

Political Participation

In simple language, political participation refers to those voluntary activities by which the members of a society take part in the selection of rulers at different levels of the government, directly or indirectly associate themselves in the process of formulating a public policy. Political participation is an essential element of the political system. Among other things, it involves voting at the polls and participation in political party activities. It is an integral part of the democratic political system. Participation of more people in the political processes and political institutions create a healthy system of the democracy unless they participate according to their free will. It has been observed by political scientists that maximum participation means more legitimacy to the activities of the government, thereby political stability resulting in the respect for authorities (Mukhi 1997: 254).

Participation in political process has been subject of abiding interest in Political Science since the days of Plato. Aristotle defined citizen as one who takes part in the administration of the justice and holds office. Declaration of French Revolution (1789) also declares that all the citizens have right to take part personally or by their representatives in the formulation of law. Marx argued that universal participation is a means and an end of the manifestation of the human freedom. The behavioural revolution which rejuvenated the academic discipline of Political Science in fifties and sixties of the nineteenth century, concentrated on the study of political behaviour, voting behaviour and electoral process. In the context of voting behaviour, the term 'political participation' has acquired new and more dynamic connotation (Patni 1994: 87). Political participation is not mere participation in the formal political processes, e.g. electoral processes. According to Pluralists decision-making is a process that involves formal and informal activities. It is not mere participation in the electoral process, participation involves participation in the meetings, involvement in election compaigning process, participation in NGO activities etc. Participation process broadly consists of all these activities which influence the decision-making process. From their perspective political participation involves numerous process through which people have their role as political participants. It is a wide process which includes numerous activities those affect the legislative, executive and judicial system. It may consist of individual activities or group activities. Participation and its modes change with the change in technology and demographic patterns also. With the awareness and educational growth of the masses, political participation increases and becomes more effective. Good example in case of India is rising female voter turnout in the elections. Use of mass media also determines the nature of the participation. With the constitutional status to the PRIs political participation has increased tremendously. At the village level, rural masses participate in the formal institutions and informal participation in the electoral meetings, in awareness drives, ward meetings, direct contact with local leaders this changed the condition that was prevailing before the 73rd Amendment. In India, to understand the political participation it requires proper understanding of demography, working of formal and informal power structures.

Denial of the participation to the people in the political system leaves no other way out but to resort to the violent methods for bringing about a change. Today, even military dictators and totalitarian states make some arrangements for the people's participation in the system in a limited way. There is some semblance of approval of their action by the people to pose to be their concerns for the people's will. In democracy, the term political participation stands for the approval and withdrawal by the people to those whom they have given right to govern. It implies that rulers shall rule only with the consent of the people and masses must be taken into confidence while performing the duties for the welfare of the society and people. Welfare state stands for the system where the policy-programmes are decided with the direct or indirect consent of the people. Questions why and how political institutions are made to undertake different types of decisions/actions to be answered to the masses by their leaders. Democracy is recognised as the best system of the governance in most of the parts of the world in present days. Democracy is twisted by the leadership of different countries according to their own needs. Most of the state leaderships try to justify their systems as democratic. Communist countries of the world plead for their system as democratic on the basis of mass participation in electoral process as voters. Political participation varies from one country to the other country. In nutshell, political participation is a process through which masses involve in the political institutions and processes. Political participation by the masses through various modes legitimises the decision-making process and helps to sustain the political system.

Difference in the level of the political participation in the democratic system is caused due to the variations in the social, economic and cultural conditions prevailing in the different societies. It is not only constitutional provisions/reservation policy that brings the masses up to the top level of the political participation. Participation is also determined by the variables like education, family system, economic structures, economic conditions, health, political awareness, political enthusiasm, culture and tradition, etc. Difference in the political participation in the developed and developing countries is the result of the difference in the forgoing variable. Within the country also political participation varies from one region to the other. Socio-cultural factors sometimes play important role. It is not possible to generalise or homogenise the political participation.

Political participation in a democratic system is known by many parameters. Most acceptable parameters of political participation are: (i) voting at the polls; (ii) participation in pre-election propaganda activities; (iii) participation in different activities of political parties; (iv) membership in related pressure groups; (v) activating political parties and pressure groups; (vi) maintaining contact with the legislators or ministers; (vii) offering oneself as a candidate for the election; (viii) holding press conference; (ix) arranging demonstration; and (x) forming trade union and arranging strikes. *International Encyclopedia of Social Sciences* refer political participation to those voluntary activities by which members of the society share in the selection of rulers directly or indirectly in the formation of public policy (Palmer 1976. 50 57). Within India, there are variations in the political participation. In some states political participation of the women as voters is high, in other states it is low. Women participation as contestants is very low in most of the states and their strength in state assemblies and Parliament is not more than ten per cent. Women participation in meetings, demonstration has been increasing day by day in rural areas. With the implementation of the New Panchayati Raj (NPR) participation, paradigms have changed to large extent.

Modes of Political Participation

There are different ways and modes through which citizens participate in politics. These modes differ from citizen to citizen in how and to what extent they participate and what are the purposes of their participation. Political acts could be hierarchically organised from the least difficult to the most difficult (Milbrath and Goel 1977: 18–19). Verba and Nie grouped the activities by which citizens can participate in politics into four broad modes of participation, i.e. voting activities, campaign activities, co-operative activities and citizen initiated contacts (Verba and Nie 1972: 47). Schonfeld has mentioned ten types of activities, which are often cited in the literature on political participation. These include: (i) running or holding, public or party office; (ii) belonging to party or other political organisation; (iii) working in an election; (iv) attending political meeting or rallies; (v) making financial contribution to a party or a candidate; (vi) contacting a public official; (vii) publicly expressing a political opinion to convince others; (viii) taking part in political discussion; (ix) voting and (x) exposing oneself to political stimuli (Schonfeld 1975: 136–37). According to Sethi, participation in political process includes all the activities, e.g. attending public meetings, taking part in the agitation activities, attendance at study circles of political parties, voting in election, participation in election campaign, membership of political party, membership of pressure groups and membership in representative bodies, etc. (Sethi 1988: 65).

Voting is considered as the simplest political activity that does not require much information and motivation as do most other political activities. Since a vote determines who holds elective public office, it exerts a pressure upon the leaders and is called as the blunt instrument of control over the government. Campaign activities require much initiative and have more collective effect upon decision-making process than voting. Membership in political party or voluntary organisation is the co-operative mode of political participation. This mode of participation requires much initiative on the part of citizens. Contesting elections is considered as the highest and most serious form of political participation than other modes of political participation. Protest activities, such as marches, rallies, strikes and other such direct actions which are called unconventional method of political participations are generally considered as unhealthy for democracy (Jharta 1998: 15–16). But slowly and gradually, this type of participation is gaining ground in many developing countries of the world. This kind of participation has immense impact on the decision-making at different levels of the government.

Variables of Political Participation

Political participation is a complex process influenced by various variables or stimuli such as socio-economic, psychological and political. It is a dependent variable which depends upon various independent variables. These variables motivate or obstruct political participation of the people. Lane observed that socio-economic difference contributes relevantly to adult participation in politics. According to him, political participation is a function of age, sex, education and status. He also refers to its complex relation to race, religion and national origin. Huntington and Dominguez established that the level of political participation tend to vary with socio-economic status (Huntington and Dominguez 1975: 33). Milbrath and Geol exhibit that the socio-economic status is positively related to unconventional political activities. Socio-economic variables include education, occupation, income, age, religion, race, sex, family background, mobility and residence. The authors have reported that people of higher socio-economic status, especially those having higher education, are more likely to be involved in politics. Political participation in the middle age is higher and it declines in old age. The married persons have reported more participation in politics than that by single persons. The author identified men's participation to be higher than that of women.

In relation to cross national comparison the male and female gap was found to be the smallest in the United States and the largest in India, with Japan, Austria and Nigeria falling between (Milbrath and Geol 1977: 92). It has been found that upper status citizens have time, money and information to be effective in politics and there is a close relation between socio-economic position and political activity (Verba and Nie 1972: 130). Rising women voter turnout also strengthens the given view that literacy, social exposer, legal equality plays important role in deciding the nature of the participation.

Further, the political behaviour is a learnt behaviour and education plays vital role in shaping it. Occupation and residence also play very important role in the political participation. Persons of the higher occupational status and urban dwellers have been reported to participate more in politics. Education is an important variable to influence groups and their level and extent of participation. Political parties often attempt to increase the participation of inactive groups. Political parties help citizens to interpret political information and event. The articulate parties have high rate of people's participation. A personal contact with party workers is more impressive way to vote or participate. Party identification also reflects the participation and it has an independent effect on participation and also reduces participation disparity between social groups. Clarity and attractiveness of issues mainly affect the election day turnout and other political activities. Flow of propaganda also influences the participation. Political development and modernisation change the participatory patterns in new nations. More modernised societies have higher political participation level than that of the less modernised ones (Milbrath and Geol 1977: 102).

The intensity of political participation in the industrialised, urbanised and complex societies is higher than in the less developed, agricultural, rural and more primitive economic and social systems. In most of the countries people with higher education, income and occupational status tend to be more involved in the politics than those who are less endowed with these attributes. The organisational involvement also leads to the political participation. Social status also promotes participation primarily through changes in attitude about politics (Huntington and Dominguez 1975: 33).

Nature and process of political participation varies from society to society. It is not only the institutional arrangements those decide the level of the political participation. Informal processes such as the traditional cultural ethos, economic status are the determinant of the political participation of the people. With the passage of the time traditional and modern variables overlap and influence the process of the political participation in all the societies.

Women's Participation in Political Processes

Generally participation of women in the political processes implies the degree of the equality and freedom enjoyed by the women in shaping and sharing of the powers and value that is given by the society to the role which their male counterparts enjoy. Political participation of women does not only mean women's participation in electoral and administrative process, but it also includes the whole range of the voluntary activities which has a bearing on the political process including voting, supporting political groups, communicating with legislators, disseminating political views and opinion among the electorates and other related activities.

Political participation of the women is an important determinant of their modernisation. It enables women to come out of the shackles of the tradition and secluded life. It also leads to greater social and political awareness among the women. Women in politics can effectively represent opinions of the other women and can also understand and deal effectively with the problems of the society and of the women in particular. Political participation of the women equips them with political competence, organisational abilities and belief in egalitarianism and democratic planning. Women's role in politics is very less than that of men although there are many qualified women who can take more political responsibilities than what is commonly believed. This political subjection is more due to the prejudice against leadership role.

After the Independence, Constitution of India made provision for equal rights to both the sexes. After the enforcement of Indian Constitution in 1947, equality of both the sexes has been maintained by providing equal opportunity to both men and women in the democratic political process. Besides constitutional provisions the question of the participation of the women in the democratic political process at large remained in the background (Singh 2007: 375). Reservation is one of the instruments of the political empowerment as it guarantees representation after the 73rd and 74th Constitutional Amendments. These can be considered as the greatest event for the women empowerment as it entailed that the one-third of the seats are reserved for women in local bodies initially when the amendment was passed. Later it was raised to 50 per cent in 2008.

Besides the electoral system, the overall political atmosphere in the country discourages women from participating in the politics. Women have relatively less ability to use money, muscle power and other forms of influence in the public sphere. Criminalisation of politics and the rising tide to violence have further discouraged the women to participate in politics at different levels. This exposure of the Indian women to greater insecurity, corruption and criminalisation has resulted in their aversion for the political scene.

Women remain at the periphery of the power structure. They lack the political consciousness needed to formulate and implement policies in accordance with the aspirations of women. Their presence is a mere symbolism rather than real power wielding. A successful democracy requires a participant society in which power is shared and authoritative decisions are made by representatives of all the citizens. Indian democracy, unfortunately, lacks the effective participation of all its citizens (Khanna 2009: 61). To strengthen the position of the women in society, equal participation of men and women is required in all the institutions. This is not only a demand of simple justice or democracy, but necessary condition for the human existence. Entry of women into politics and decision-making structures can lead to the holistic transformation. They can redefine political priorities and place new items on the political agenda to address gender specific concerns and provide a new perspective on the mainstream political issues. Women have long been overlooked in the process of development. It is also necessary to overcome the patriarchal orientations of the society. Education, development of scientific outlook, legal safeguards, enlightenment of men and awareness of their own potential by women are the effective forces in this direction (Khanna 2009: 62).

Securing the participation of women in the institutions of democracy and governance is now an important item on the global agenda. According to Census 2011, women population in 586.46 million, representing 48.46 per cent of country's population of 1,210.19 million. Development of women has always been the major thrust area in the development planning since independence. In the first twenty years, policy makers were primarily concerned with overall economic growth. The third decade after the independence witnessed an increase in the concerns for equity and poverty alleviation. From 1990 onward, the focus has been on the empowerment of the women.

India has heralded the new millennium by pronouncing the year 2001 as Women's Empowerment Year. In terms of political empowerment, nearly seven lakh women occupy positions as members and chairpersons of grassroots democratic institutions in India, following the reservation clause in 73rd and 74th Amendments, providing one-third seats at district, *taluk*, village and municipal level for women. This is for the first time in our history that an opportunity has been provided for substantial entry of the women in the public life and a large number of women have come forward to tackle the challenge of the leadership at all levels of the Panchayats. In fact, right from the days of the freedom struggle the Indian women have been consistently encouraged to take part in the active politics. Vitiated political milieu affected women political participation adversely, despite the fact that there has been a marked increase in the literacy levels and political awareness among women. It is recognised that the goal of the poverty alleviation is difficult to achieve without the role and active participation of the women, who constitute a large section of the workforce in the country. Women's empowerment is critical to the process of the development of the community and, therefore, bringing them into the mainstream of development has been a major concern of the government (Pargunan 2008: 61).

In the present times, there is a growing consciousness to recognise women's autonomy and their capacity to act as 'full citizens'. Their role in the social, political and economic context needs to be recognised in the right earnest and the forces that keep the women away from the mainstream need to be countered. Women can be effective agents of change and important contributors to the national development. Their status can be co-related to their participating rights and obligations in managing the society. The significant indicators of the status of women in any society are political participation, representation and share the decision-making bodies. Representation of the women is considered important both for the normative and practical reasons. Viewed from the normative perspective, the interests of all the citizens should be represented by the political elite (Nefrusturna 2000: 125). If women are not included in the political process it may result in policies reflecting only the male perspective. Thus, practically, it may lead to the allocation of resources and decisions in such a way which may not be in the interest of women (Counell 1990: 507).

Indian Constitution brought legal equality. Constitutional provisions and legislative securities subsequently led women to leave the relative calm of private life and enter both elective and appointive public offices in unprecedented numbers. India has the distinction of having lady Prime Minister for nearly twenty years and several women Chief Ministers and Governors at the state level. Reservation of 33 per cent seats for the women in the Panchayats (local government) and a proposal for a similar reservation in the Parliament, all these developments raised hope for the betterment of women. However, this was only an illusion, which camouflaged reality. In general, the involvement of the women in politics has been low key. They form part of the syndrome of exclusion from political power. Its evidence is poor representation in political parties, parliament and state legislatures. Their share in administration is also meagre.

Traditionally, women have been volunteers in civic and social community efforts, in electoral politics as political wives, party loyalists and voters. In political decision-making their status has been subordinate to that of men. Only a small section of women belonging to or supported by affluent and influential families have managed to enter the political mainstream. In general, they cast their vote and take part in agitational political activities but lag behind in enjoying positions of power and decision-making. This is evident in the formal political institutions at the states and national level.

Tribal Women and Political Status

Theoretically, the low status of women has been accepted in a majority of the tribal societies. But still according to Dhebar Commission Report (1961), the tribal woman, in most of the cases is not a dredge or a beast of burden but exercises a firm hand in the family matters. Tribal women in matriarchal and matrilineal societies are undoubtedly better off in comparison to the tribal women in patriarchal and patrilineal societies.

Tribal women as a whole seem to enjoy comparatively more freedom and are devoid of many constraints that imposed caste on Hindu women. They might lead a very hard life as far as physical labour is concerned but they certainly enjoy more freedom than their counterparts among the caste Hindus. They can roam about freely, visit markets or friends, cut jokes with men without reservations and are usually free to select their life partners. Many of them can divorce and remarry without social sanctions (Thakur 1996: 5). Tribal women's position is better than the mainstream society. In tribal politics and in the formal political institutions tribal women also have same fortune which the women from general category are enjoying as privilege being the part of political families.

Issues of Caste and Class

In common parlance, a caste is an elaborate and complex social system that combines elements of occupation, endogamy, culture, social class, tribal affiliation and political power. It should not be confused with more elementary aspects such as nobility, race or social class, in that members of all the castes in one society may or may not belong to the same race, whilst members of the same clan or nobility, in the same society, may be of different race and or caste. Although Indian society is often now associated with the word 'caste', it was first used by the Portuguese to describe inherited class status in their own European society (Jone 2013: 1).

Caste system dates almost 3,000 years back and caste setup was formed to provide base to form a social order in the ancient India. Traditional system in India was organised around the caste structure and caste identities (Kothari 1970: 4). Caste, rather than caste system in India has played an important role in the polity of the country for so many centuries. Most developed form of the caste system occurs in India (Sharma 1993: 1). Caste and caste system has been defined by the scholars of different disciplines. For Hutton (1964: 50) 'Caste is an endogamous group often with an ascribed occupation and ranked relative to other castes'. Leach views castes as 'an organic system with each particular caste and sub-caste feeling a distinctive functional role. It is a system of labour division from which the element of the competition among the workers has been largely excluded' (Leach 1960: 10). Some of the sociologist refute the Leach's idea of non-competition and opine 'castes do compete between each other for acquiring political and economic power and high ritual position' (Srinivas 1962: 15). Eminent Indian sociologist defined caste as endogamous usually localised group, having traditional association with an occupation and a particular position in hierarchy of castes. Relations between castes are governed among other things, by the concepts of pollution and purity and generally maximum commensality occurs within the castes' (Srinivas, op. cit., 23). Typical Indian social system based on the caste system was fragmented relatively closed social groups, hierarchically arranged, each associated with a particular set of privileges and disabilities those were supported by traditional sections. These status groups wee castes and it was caste which ordered intervals and attitudes. Different castes were rigidly separated from one another by the economic activities, rituals and social barriers. Position of the caste in the ritual hierarchy largely corresponded with its position in the economic and political sphere. But the caste is neither unique nor it is static, unchangeable and immutable as it often assumed. It is rather fluid and mutable. These characteristics make caste or more *Jati* one of the vital and dynamic identities Indian society and politics' (Hauser 1997: 48). Caste institution in Indian system has dominant position. It always had prime position in determining the Indian system inclusively.

After Independence, with the democratisation of the Indian polity, involvement of the traditional institutions and processes in Indian politics became significant development of the Indian system. Caste system made available to the leadership, structural ideological bases for the political mobilisation, providing it with both segmental organisation and identification system, on which support could be crystallised (Kothari, op. cit., 13). Caste became the base of the Indian political leadership after independence, with regard to which the leadership was forced to make concession to local opinion, take its candidates from consensus that existed as regards claim to power, articulate competition on traditional lines and in turn, organise castes for economic and political purposes' (Srinivas 1962: 46). Jawaharlal Nehru, who is known as the architect of the Indian polity, failed to evolve successful policy to de-insitutionalise caste as base for the political system. Political parties always engage themselves in the manipulation of the caste based politics to earn electoral benefits in India.

Caste system influences the power structures and roles in the tribal societies also. They have their own distinct caste system. Socio-economic and political system of the tribal's is also based on the caste practices. It is still prevalent as part of India's society. Having been around for centuries, it is highly doubtful that caste system will die out completely. Its presence in the politics is persistence and its role changes with the change in the political development.

Caste and class are viewed as the two most significant dimensions of social stratification. They are considered as closely interrelated, almost inseparable, basic processes of social life. It is one thing that caste is viewed as a role model for analysing Indian society or class is used for analysing caste and power, but it is quite different in real life as caste and class are not only highly differentiated internally, complexities of their expertness and articulation signify the vast ramifications of structured social inequality. Debate on caste and class has covered wide-range of issues related to the indicators of status, levels of equality and inequality, cultural and structural interaction, occupational mobility, etc. (Sharma 2010: 1). Caste is the development of thousands of years, from the amalgamation of many different racial and other groups in a single cultural system. Caste is not merely a social imitation but part of Hinduism, which on that account has been described as a socio-religious system, for it is partly a social organisation and partly a religious belief, or congeries of beliefs. Caste is, in fact, the steel frame binding together the many beliefs massed together in Hinduism. So it is integral part of Hinduism (Devi 1999: 9).

Tribes

The social thinkers consider the 'Tribe' as a social group usually with a definite area, dialect, cultural homogeneity and unifying social organisation. It can include several sub groups such as clans or sibs. A Tribe ordinarily has an ancestor and its own deity. The families and groups composing the larger tribal units are linked through 'blood ties' as the term is commonly used and through 'religious, social and socio-economic functions' (Khan 2000: 2).

According to *Encyclopedia Britannica,* 'tribe' is termed as a 'small group defined by traditions of common descent and having temporary or permanent political integration above the family level and a similar language, culture and ideology' (Britannica: 918). Term 'Scheduled Tribe' is of recent origin and came into existence by the Constitution of India adopted on 26 January 1950. Prior to that they were called by various names such as 'Aboriginals', 'Adivasis', 'Forest Tribes', 'Hill Tribes' and 'Primitive Tribes'. Up to 1919 they were included in the category of the backward classes under the head of 'Depressed Classes' and within this category following sub-categories were included:

1. Criminals and Wandering Tribes,
2. Aboriginal Tribes, and
3. Untouchables (Ghurye 1943: 21).

In Census 1931, the term 'Primitive Tribes' was used to specify the tribal population of India who were used to be called as 'Forest Tribes' or 'Hill Tribes'. But in Census 1941 they were simply termed as 'Tribe'. But nowadays in the Indian Constitution, the tribes are scheduled and popularly termed as 'Scheduled Tribes' (Khan 2000: 4). Term Tribe commonly signifies a group of people speaking a common language, observing uniform rules of social organisation and working together for common purposes. The other typical characteristics of Tribe include a common name, a contiguous territory, a relatively uniform culture or way of life and a tradition of common descent. According to another contention, Tribe is generally used to denote a group of primitive or barbarous clans under recognised chiefs (*Encyclopedia of Primitive Tribes in India*, Vol. 1: 2004). Scheduled Tribe (ST) as term first appeared in the Constitution of India. Article 366(25) defined Scheduled Tribe as 'such tribes or tribal communities or parts of or groups within such tribes or tribal communities as are deemed under Article 342 to be Scheduled Tribes for the purposes of this Constitution' (Ministry of Tribal Affairs).

Many tribes very often live by hunting, fishing or gathering. The aboriginal inhabitants of the Andaman Islands, however, depend upon these activities for their livelihood. They have no trade relation with others and are much isolated from one another that the Onges of little Andaman do not understand the language of the Jarawas of the Great Andaman or of the inhabitants of the North sentinel island, all of which are close by. In the midst of warm, rain drenched forests of Tripura, Manipur, Nagaland, Mizo district and NEFA, there live a number of tribal communities who depend principally upon a rather simple form of cultivation. The same method is also in vogue among some of the tribes of the Orissa and Madhya Pradesh.

It is almost obvious that the tribal communities in India are extremely backward and poverty stricken. It is because a number of communities have continued in the pastoral or shifting cultivation stage of the economy till today. Agriculture in the tribal region remained backward because of poor pace of infrastructure growth in this areas. Tribal economy is intimately connected with the forests economy. Tribal population in India belongs to the various stages of the cultural development. Though, tribal culture differs from tribe to tribe. Tribes in India find pleasure with activities such as singing, dancing, drinking, story-telling, etc. through cycles of festivals and their happy-go lucky spontaneous nature sharply contrast to non tribal counterparts in the country. Most of the tribals in India have rich tradition of oral literature. Tribal religion in India seems to have a common feature, that all beings are endowed with a living spirit. Animals, plants, rivers, mountains are no exception to this rule (Thakur 1986: 26–27)

There are about 705 (Census 2011) tribes and sub-tribes in different parts of the country. Barring Haryana, Jammu and Kashmir, Punjab, Chandigarh, Delhi and Pondicherry, all other states and union territories have Scheduled Tribe population. Madhya Pradesh, Orissa, Bihar and Rajasthan account for more than 50 per cent of the entire

Scheduled Tribe population in the country. As a matter of tradition, the tribals have inhabited isolated areas. Due to a very difficult and inhospitable terrain and total absence of the communication facilities, the tribals led a secluded life without any contact with the outside world for several centuries. Primitive modes and unsophisticated techniques of production, lack of infrastructural facilities coupled with utter ignorance thrust upon them abysmal poverty, backwardness and ill-health which persisted for several centuries.

After the independence, the tribal societies in the country have also witnesses to several drastic changes. These changes came about because of the impact of various policy initiatives and welfare measures of the government. The Constitution of India assigns the responsibility of the socio-economic development of the weaker sections of the society, particularly the Scheduled Castes and Scheduled Tribes, to the Government of India. The advent of planned development in 1960s gave a new lease of life to the poverty stricken tribals. The successive Five Year Plans had drawn up several special programmes and schemes for the development of tribal areas and also the people inhabiting these areas and necessary funds were allocated for their implementation. Adoption of strategic sub-plan has resulted in the growth of administrative apparatus in the tribal areas which proved beneficial for these areas (Tribal Sub-Plan). Nehru's approach was based on the development of all the sections of society, irrespective of caste, colour, gender and domicile. The areas of his vision of development were more wider and diverse, from fostering human dignity, world peace, democracy, planning and development, socialism, secularism, Indian nationhood. His vision was dominated by the wider goals. His focus diluted the aspirations of the natives. Masses always aspired in the past to strengthen their systems (socio, economic and political) according to their ways. Rath (2006: 92) commented Nehru was not able to understand Elwin concept of tribal autonomy, which created confusion in the policy making process of free India.

In the tribal political life there have been several drastic changes after independence. During the post-independence period mainly two significant developments have taken place in the tribal political system. Democracy which was ushered in the country granted several political rights to the tribal along with all the other section in the society. It provided an opportunity to the tribals to share political power with others. Constitution of India through the Articles 330, 332 and 334 reserved seats in the Parliament and the State Assemblies for the Scheduled Tribes and the Scheduled Castes. Through the reservation system they got the chance of contesting the elections and enter the legislative bodies to share the political power with the non-tribals (Narayan 1992: 5). Indian tribal concerns in the Indian Constitution (1950) served as a beacon for the international community. UNO and ILO also recognised importance of the 'indigenous people' and UN made its Declaration on the Rights of Indigenous People in its 36th meeting on August 1994, which contained 45 Articles covering their right to culture, education, health, territory, development political autonomy and so on. PESA Act of 1996 on the lines of 73rd Amendment covers directly or indirectly almost all the provisions related to the Rights of Indigenous people under taken by the 36th meeting of UNO 1994. Indian government always give due weightage to the UNO initiatives to maintain a harmonious relationship within the country as well as on the international level among the world community.

Tribal areas of the Himachal Pradesh constitute 42.5 per cent of the state's geographical area. 5.7 per cent of the state's total population is the tribal population. Kinnaur and Lahaul Spiti districts, Pangi, Bharmaur *tehsil* of Chamba district constitute states tribal area. More than sixty per cent of the total tribal population of the state lives in these areas.

Tribals of the Himachal Pradesh are divided into two main categories on the basis of their language and religion. Gaddi, Pangwals and Swangla are mainly from the Hindu fold practicing Hinduism blended with local traditions. They worship the deities of Hindu pantheon and Lord Shiva is their chief deity. The Bhots or Bodhs are also small tribal community inhabiting Lahaul-Spiti, Kinnaur, Kullu and Shimla. They are scattered and are not easy to be located for the purpose of in-depth study since they are Buddhist by faith, their cultural traditions have got assimilated in the vast *triratna* of Dharma, Sangha, and the Buddha. Like other tribals of the state, they are religious minded and follow the principles of the Buddhism in letter and spirit (Sharma 2010: 423).

In the agro-pastoral economy of the tribal areas of Himachal Pradesh where the mechanisation of agricultural operations is not possible, cattle are kept not only for providing nutritious food, such as milk and butter, but also for valuable draught power and manure which are essential for agriculture in the region. Sheep and goats are reared for wool and meat. Livestock rearing has been and is still one of the main pillars of tribal economy as it provides subsidiary means of livelihood to the farmers (Sharda and Sharma 1998).

Present work is multi-disciplinary focused on different dimensions, issues, and problems relating to the tribal society of India. Within the tribal India diversity cannot be overlooked. Each tribal segment has its own distinct socio-cultural, economic and political identity. Distinction among them is mainly caused by the geographical and local variables. After independence, various steps have been taken by the successive governments to bring them parallel to the mainstream population by special efforts without intervening with their age old ethnicity. In this field in the broader perspective 73rd Amendment and particularly PESA Act are the landmark initiatives. Provisions under the Act provide enough space to the tribal communities to balance the 'tradition with modernity'. Legislative measures act like a structure. For its successful implementation comprehensive ground work is required. It includes proper orientation of all the stake holders, genuine will of the political leadership and the sincere efforts of the implementing agencies (bureaucracy). Work deals with these dimensions.

The year 1991 is taken as the benchmark year. Government of India's initiative of New Economic Policy (NEP 1991) let the corporate enter into the remote tribal areas. Application of the concept of the NEP affected the tribal community in all parts of the country. In 1993 Seventy Third Amendment was passed to strengthen the grassroots democracy. On lines of the Amendment under the PESA Act 1996, PRIs Systems extended to the tribal areas of Schedule V of the Indian Constitution. For this purpose various variable economic disparities, the changing scenario of agriculture and forestry in tribal areas, certain aspects of environmental demography, nature and instruments of the social transformation including education and cooperatives, tribal customs, traditions, religion and folk music, myths and realities about the tribes and tribal areas were part of the study.

Methodology

The study is conducted through combination of three paradigm and new positive, interactive and critical realist. The tribal societies have composite system. Without understanding one sub system it is not possible to analyse one another. Hence, historical, sociological, anthropological descriptive approaches are adopted to understand the political structures, institutions and processes. To explore the impact of various variables such as class, caste, gender sociological and anthropological approaches are also adopted.

2

Decentralisation and Local Self Government

Decentralisation is generally defined as a process whereby administrative authority, public resources and responsibilities are devolved and delegated from the central or state government agencies to the lower level institutions such as the village panchayats, municipalities and non-governmental organisations (NGOs). This kind of a system develops a people centric system of the governance that enables hitherto powerless individuals and groups to play significant role in the implementation of the programmes policies and mobilisation, allocation and distribution of the public resources. They become engines of the development and not merely its beneficiaries. Its main purpose is to bring accountability in the governance ensuring economic and social justice (Singh and Misra 1993: 4). Decentralisation facilitates the development on the principles of the democracy where the people have right to decide their own fortune.

In Indian context 73rd and 74th Amendment (1993) stands for the participation of the people in the decision-making process, with the focus on the newly created organisations, institutions and agencies (PRIs and Municipal bodies). Dispersal of the control over power is the main concern of the decentralisation. Local Self Government is an essential attribute of the democratic decentralisation. It can be described as that form of the government under which the people of various locations possess certain responsibilities and exercise of discretion in the administration of the local affairs. Local self government has existed in India since the ancient times. Vedas, Puranas, Smritis, the state craft and religious texts contain vivid description of the local institutions.

'Grassroots democracy is neither a new concept nor it is an expression of the Western political thought operationalised in Indian soil. Origin of the grassroots level democracy dates back to the Vedic age and has been well documented in the ancient scriptures such as Rig Veda, Aitareya Brahman, Panini's Ashtadhyai, Kautilyas Arthasastra, inscriptions on Ashoka's pillars and writing of the Buddhist and Jain scholars'. Village was the cardinal institution of the Indian governance structures. During the Muslim rulers, no drastic change in the structure was traceable in the village system. Before the advent of British colonisers, Indian political history substantiate the view that the central power tried to consolidate the Indian sub-continent under the centralised system under the different rulers. Their efforts failed to displace the indigenous system. Before the Britishers came India's Polity had federal nature village was the primary unit of governance. Centralised system introduced by the Britishers to serve their own interests.

The arrival of the British as traders and their subsequent transformation into the ruling class, marked a significant period in socio-political history. They tried to rebuild Indian society to serve their vested interests. Their vice like grip over administrative affairs of the country ensured that they were in a position to manipulate the system in a manner that suited them. Being traders in the early days and later on as colonisers, they exploited the Indian social-economic system according to their own interests. For that purpose they disturbed the Indian village and indigenous system of Panchayats. They introduced an administrative system based on the bureaucratic principles governed by Max Weber's 'Bureaucratic Model'. Officials had scant concern towards the existing indigenous system. The new system was based on the hierarchical order, masses were treated as commodities humane factors being the major casualty. Only those Indians who gave preference to British interests over nationalistic feelings were rewarded. Their objective was mere revenue collection and to dislodge the age old Indian economy, to get maximum economic benefits for their own economy. The new institutions introduced by the British lacked democratic spirit. Their imperial orientation to exploit the natives was conspicuously dominant. They tried to consolidate their position at any cost; 1773 to 1892, system of the governance was totally dominated by the centralised principles. They enacted different Acts and tried to consolidate the power system in their favour. In 1892, representation in the provincial council was given to the Indians. The ruling class enjoyed supremacy in the governance. Indians were not entrusted with greater responsibilities in the governing institutions even after 1892. In the late nineteenth century, Lord Ripon made some efforts to strengthen the municipal bodies, although no attention was still being paid to the rural local bodies. In 1907 Commission on Decentralisation was constituted due to the rising pressures and awakening of the Indians. The ensuring Acts of 1909, 1919 and 1935 were actuated by the motive of pacifying the rising voices of discontent. Some of the leaders during the national movement not only opposed the British, they also demanded restructuring of the Indian political institutions in tune with the age old indigenous practices. They also demanded decentralisation based on the federal principles. Act of 1935 recognises the federal polity: distribution of powers, strong position of the provinces in the federal polity. Local government could not get proper attention of leaders during the national movement. In nutshell, Britishers moulded the system according to own priorities. Little attention was paid to strengthening of Panchayats as primary institutions of the local self governance. Indian 'Village System' faced challenges from the transformations brought by the British in totality. Thus, an age old institution, the pillar of Indian socio-economic and political system lost its sheen by the time India attained Independence.

Dawn of freedom created the hope that the concept of 'decentralised governance' will regain its lost glory through the institutionalisation of Mahatma Gandhi's idea of 'Gram Swaraj' by creating a polity that will ensure maximum power with the Panchayats and minimum power with the Central Government. In Gandhiji's vision, the Indian independence must begin at the bottom where every village will be a republic and Panchayats will have full power (Singh 2007: 15). According to Gandhi, 'The picture of village Sawaraj is not resurrection of the old village Panchayats but the fresh formation of independent village units of Swaraj in the context of present world'.

Local self governance, initially in the Indian Constitution, had an insignificant position in Article 40 of the Indian Constitution under 'Directive Principles of the State Policy' which envisages, 'the state shall take step to organise village Panchayats and endow them with such power and authority as may be necessary to enable them to function as a unit of self government'. Initially, focus of the architects of 'future India' was to build Indian democracy based on the Parliamentary form of government. Representative institutions were restricted to the national and states level. Their understanding of the Indian society and its ethos misconceived. Democratic paradigms evolved in the early years led to the gap between perception and practice. Dream of mass democracy somehow deviated towards the idea of the elite democracy. The sole part of the masses in the Indian democracy was reduced to elect MLAs and MPs. Their involvement in state building, nation building and in development process was negligible. Bureaucracy was all pervasive, development without proper understanding of the local needs and expectations of the masses was considered their sole aim. With this approach in the early years after independence different programmes were launched for the development of the village society of the India. Community Development Programme (CDP) was first such programme. It was launched in 1952 to strengthen the rural community. Its planning and execution was the sole responsibility of the government institutions. After five years of its implementation, it was realised that without people's participation the goal of the community development could not be achieved. A comprehensive review of the local government and administration in India conducted by Balwant Rai Mehta (BRM) study team in the year 1957 envisaged a 'three tier' system of the decentralisation, namely the village Panchayat, the Panchayat Samiti and Zila Parishad. The system proposed by the committee was aimed to enhance the mass participation in the development in democratic way. Basic principles of the democratic decentralisation recommended by the committee were also endorsed by the National Development Council (NDC) in 1958. This paved the way for the constitution of the Panchayati Raj Institutions in all the states. Rajasthan was the first state to implement the Panchayati Raj on the basis of the recommendations of the Mehta Committee. Contemporary Prime Minister Jawaharlal Nehru inaugurated the first Panchayati Raj System on 2 October 1959 at Nagaur in Rajasthan. However, Mehta Committee recommendations were not implemented in the letter and spirit. Nehru made some efforts after his death leadership got entangled in consolidation of the power at the centre level. In late sixties and seventies, emergence of first generation regional parties and their demand for more powers to the states and Mrs Indira Gandhi's ambition for concentration of the power at highest two contradictory positions created tough situation for the decentralisation of the power till the grassroots level.

Indian federalism in practice emerged as the centrifugal system. The dominance of the one party, at the centre and at the state level marginalised the process of the decentralisation. Local government was virtually non-existing system. Elections for these bodies were highly irregular. Local elites had dominant position in the institutions where they existed in different parts of the country. Concrete steps were not taken at the national and state level to consolidate the local bodies. Lack of decentralisation and empowerment to plan and implement the development programmes led to the lopsided development and struggle for more federalisation in the form of rise of the regional parties (DMK in Tamil Nadu and Akali Dal in Punjab) as effective medium to aggregate the local interests. Emergence of the centrifugal forces resulted into demand for the change in the governing pattern also. These parties strongly demanded autonomy to the states from different platforms. Their logic was that the state should be powerful enough to serve diverse interests. In mid seventies, JP Movement for the total revolution also represented cause of the decentralisation. Movement also represented the view of ideologues of the different ideologies; Ram Manohar Lohia (Socialist), Deendayal Upadhayaya (Jan Sangh). The result of these developments was change of government at the centre in 1977 by the Janta Coalition which was heterogeneous coalition of the socialist, rightist and centre rightist parties made an endeavour to review the existing system. Ashok Mehta Committee was set up to look into the matter and suggest measures for effective local governing system. The Committee proposed two tier system at the block and district level. Zila Parishad constituted at the district level and Mandal Panchayat at the block level consisting of a group of villages covering population of the 15,000 to 20,000. Recommendations were made to ensure the representation of the SC and ST through reservation, regular elections for the local bodies and proper utilisation of the development funds for the weaker sections of the society. In the context of providing representation to the women, it suggested that if no woman was elected, two women who would get the highest number of the votes in Zila Panchayat election should become members of the PRIs. In the event of no women coming forward for the election, two women might be co-opted. In spite all these recommendations, women's representation in all the Gram Panchayat and Zila Panchayats remained very low and their participation in the meetings and decision-making was also in proxy (Nilofer and Praveen 2008: 662). Ashok Mehta Committee was followed by G.V.K. Raw Committee (1985). Committee concluded that bureaucratisation of development administration in opposition to the democratisation and weakened the panchayati raj institutions. An important recommendation of the committee was to reserve a significant position for the local bodies in the planning process. Dr L.M. Singhvi Committee in 1987 recommended that the PRIs should be constitutionally recognised, protected and preserved by the inclusion of a new chapter in the Constitution (Dhaka 2004: 32). For a decade with the change of the leadership many committees were appointed; all of them laid emphasis on the importance of the decentralisation and effective role of the elected local bodies, to strengthen the political democracy at the grassroots level. It became clear from the development process and negligible role of the local bodies in political India that grassroots democracy is the only practical solution for filling the gaps between perceptions and practices. Thesis of all the efforts of government and non-governmental efforts to visualise the flaws in existing Indian political system was the constitutional status to the local governmental bodies.

In 1993, 73rd and 74th Amendment Acts provided constitutional recognition and status to the local elected bodies in villages (Panchayats) and cities (municipalities) respectively. Apart from putting in place institutions of local governance and decentralising power structures, the Amendments also sought to deepen the democracy by ensuring that hitherto excluded social group like women, SCs and STs (marginalised or dalits) are adequately represented in the local bodies. These Amendments are comprehensive exercise in the field of decentralisation; different clauses (periodical elections, provision of State Finance Commission, Gram Sabha) provided space for the effective local government. Provisions in the amendments widen the scope of representation to the diverse sections of the society those were on margin in the Indian social system. Democratisation of the decision-making process by strengthening the Panchayat is also land mark step in the field of participatory democracy. Shift from 'elite to mass democracy' through Gram Sabha and periodical elections served two purposes. One is, its a step to realise the dream of decentralisation of Gandhian school of thought (broadly included JP, Ram Manohar Lohia, Deen Dayal Upadhayaya), other its a step to empower those who were on the margins and were not able to contribute according to their capacity.

In 1996 Panchyats Extension to the Scheduled Areas (PESA Act 1996) was enacted to enhance the decentralisation process to the tribal areas of Schedule V. Act was formulated in accordance to the 73rd Amendment. Basic objective of the legislation is to empower the native people to decide their own ways and goals on the one hand, on the other hand to empower them to meet the growing challenges posed by the rapid changes in the era of liberalisation, globalisation and privatisation.

Tribal people have been given enormous powers through Gram Sabha to take collective decisions in the interest of community. Mass participation in the formal and informal local institutions would strengthen the democratic edifice of the Indian society. Tribal society constitutes important segment of Indian society as well as of the international community because after African continent maximum tribal population lives in India. It is desirable that tribal community should also have effective participation in the political processes.

Women who constitute 49 per cent population of the country, their participation in the political processes is not merely inevitable for the political democracy but also have importance for the establishment of a balanced society. Reservation in the local bodies provided space to the women-folk to contribute in development of the Indian society. Women political participation encourages women and develop confidence among them to take up those ventures which were traditionally considered in the male domain. Tribal women are more open and society has less constrains in case of women participation in the social and economic activities. She enjoys authority in the family affairs. In the political field tribal women are less active. They are least interested in the power politics. Their participation is confined to voting, attending the Gram Sabha meetings casually. Although tribal women cannot be ignored as important part of the society. Their equal participation in diverse political processes would protect community interest at large and tribal women interest particularly. Reservation within the PESA Act 1996 is a landmark step to involve tribal women in the political activities and harness their strengths to develop the tribal society.

Caste and class are important variables in the tribal society like mainstream and affect the political of the tribal society. Stratification among the tribes is also common. Political power at the local level is enjoyed by a particular strata this trend is also visible among the tribes after implementation of the PESA Act.

Conclusion

Democratic decentralisation, as term has popularised in India in the recent past as a process, can be traced in the ancient Indian history. Village was the unit of governance every village managed its own affairs according to its requirement and will of the community was dominating factor in the governance. Britishers focused on the consolidation and centralisation of powers to manipulate and manage their self-interest, it had negative impact on the indigenous system which was primarily based on the institution of village. For the resurgence of the decentralisation as cardinal principle of the Indian polity numerous organised and unorganised forces have played important role. 73rd Amendment of the Indian Constitution gave space for the 'decentralisation, mass participation' in rural local government.

3

Tribal Situation in India

This chapter concerns with the issues related to the conditions of the Indian tribes that account for approximately 8.6 per cent of the total population of the country. Due to their geographical conditions, poor living conditions, education and health profile on the national level, these tribes are the third most vulnerable sections of the society after the women and children. Constitution of India warrants that each and every one in the country should have liberty, equality and get social justice irrespective of the manmade differences. But the fact that inequalities in the society still exist cannot be wished away. The marginalised are far behind the mainstream population. In spite of a respectable rate of GDP in the last two decades, condition of the deprived sections has not improved much till date. Complexities resulting from the liberalisation of the economy have created added challenges for the tribals. It is imperative to understand the present predicament of the tribes and try to find out the effective remedies to get rid off their existing problems. Mega projects in the tribal areas, unscientific mining and exploitation of the water resources have disturbed their life style. 'Displacement and disturbance' has become common feature of the tribal life. This chapter is devoted to an in depth analysis of the tribal situation.

Tribal groups are presumed to from the oldest ethnological section of the national population. The term *Adivasis* (Adi: original; vasi: inhabitant) has recently gained currency, in order to designate these groups. There are numerous tribal communities in different parts of our country, and many of them still maintain their primitive culture. As they always maintained their distance from the main stream of the society, they remained socially and economically backward, in comparison to the rest of the population of the country. Scheduled Tribes (ST) of India are the earliest inhabitants or indigenous people of the country who were unable to defend themselves and were gradually forced to recede before the invading hoards of such people, as the Dravidians, Indo-Aryans and Mongols coming from the West, North-West and North-East respectively, who were not only superior in numerical strength but also in mechanical equipment. The indigenous people thus took shelter in the mountain depths and thick jungles, where a considerable number of them are still found and have been estimated to be about ten million. Those who were left behind on the plains gradually disappeared either by absorption or by acculturation (Das 1993: 13). The Aryans, Iranian invasions exercised strong influence over Punjab and North West India mentioned in Farshita's *History of the India.* Later Parthian, Saka, Yueh-chi, Chinese and Tibetian, Hun and Turk influenced the northern tribals of today (Bahadur 1978).

Term 'tribe' has certain important characteristics. Chief among them which are as under:

1. The scheduled tribes are the original inhabitants of India and amongst them some groups are very old; Generally, they prefer to remain in isolation and inhabiting either in the forest or in case of village or town, outside the village, by establishing their own community locality as a separate one;
2. their sense of history is very shallow and due to lack of education they are ignorant of their past history;
3. they have got their own language, institutions, beliefs and customs;
4. they practice primitive religion and have great faith on mythology, ghosts and witches;
5. formerly they were solely dependent on the forest produce and at present some of them are doing farming or working as labour;
6. most of them are non-vegetarians and have got the nomadic habits specially of dancing and drinking;
7. they belong to one of the three stocks – Negritos, Mongoloides and Mediterranean;
8. these people have a very low level of technical and economic development.

Tribal people who differ in physical features, talks in diverse language and belong to the different types of economic systems, starting from food gathering stage and ramifying into settled agricultural and industrial groups. These groups of people are distributed all over India (Khan 2000: 3).

Etymologically, term 'tribe' derives its origin from the word 'tribes' meaning a divining (or a pronged divining) of the roman people. Initially the term had no such pejorative as came to be assigned it later on.

It is difficult to define the term judiciously. It has been defined by the scholars according to the existing conditions and demand of the time. *Oxford Dictionary*, Vol. xi, 1933 defined a tribe as race of people now applied especially to a primary aggregate of people in a primitive or barbarous condition, under a headman or chief (p. 39). *Collins Dictionary* (1987) defines a tribe as a group of people of the same race, who share the same customs, religion, language or land, especially when they are not considered to have reached a very advanced level of civilisation (p. 156), *Webster Dictionary* (1966) mentions that a tribe is a social group comprising numerous families, clans or generations together with slaves dependents or adopted strangers (p. 945). Concept of the tribe is dynamic. It has certain common features besides its dynamic nature; they are homogeneous sub-groups comparatively lagging behind the mainstream society in the development.

In case of India, tribal society does not fit in the standardised definitions given by the different dictionaries. Terms like barbarous, primitive are not relevant in the Indian tribal context. Tribal population of India, in terms of their level of development, historical past and rich cultural heritage reflects vast divergence. This diversity among the Indian tribes pose a challenge to define tribe in the Indian context. Nehru, the first Prime Minister of India made the point clear by explaining the tribal society of India. 'Most historical writings have sought to reflect man's disunity and, therefore, much of what has been written about the tribes in the various parts of India ... . Such a colonial ethos has undermined the whole concept of the study of tribal life and this is why we do not have coherent, logical or broadly applicable definition of a 'tribe' (quoted in Gavit and Chande 1989: 140–154). According to Dube in the Indian context, the term has never been defined precisely. It was used, at time, to denote a bewildering variety of social categories that were either analogous or comparable (Gupta et al. 1998: 51). Anthropologists in particular and social scientists in general have always looked at tribes as a social type and clubbed them into particular socio-economic categories. Indian tribes have rich cultural heritage. They have distinct social set ups, more or less developed and refined according to the needs of their society. Political institutions in the tribal society are based on the principles of the direct democracy. Elder stratum of the tribal society is empowered by the community to decide contentious issues put before them by the people. Their economy is primitive, based on the forest, rearing of livestock and traditional professions (handicrafts and service providers to the community). With the changing times, a gradual change is coming about in their professional life. In the Indian Constitution, term is not defined. Tribal community of the country, is not homogeneous community. Indian tribes are heterogeneous social groups with regimental social structure and territorial affiliation. Sub-groups have a common dialect or language, and its economy is pre-industrial and not market oriented. It is governed by its hereditary political functionaries by means of customary laws, norms and values, and it maintains its socio-cultural identity by recognising social distance from other tribal groups. Given argument is still relevant in case of tribes in the country.

After independence, special steps have been taken to bring the tribes in the mainstream. Tribes have strong affinity with their culture. They are least interested in adopting the mainstream practices. It cannot be denied that the constitutional measures and government initiatives and interventions have left imprint on the tribal life. They welcome the steps those do not interfere with the cultural practices. Bhuria Committee (1994) also recognised this fact that tribal sub-groups maintain their solidarity even today and keep them separate from the other tribal groups. In cases of their social and marriage alliances, they are endogamous group. Youngsters also follow this convention to a great extend.

Difficulty in defining the Indian tribes can be largely attributed to the geographic and demographic reasons. In the Indian Constitution, certain tribes have been specified as Scheduled Tribes (ST) on the basis of certain criteria. These are: (i) traditional occupation of a definite geographical area; (ii) distinctive culture that includes the whole spectrum of tribal way of life, i.e. language, customs, traditions religious beliefs, arts and crafts, etc.; (iii) primitive trades depicting occupational patterns, economy, etc.; (iv) lack of educational and techno-economic development (Pati 2002: 13).

The largest tribal population of the world after Africa resides in India. Tribal population of India is almost equal to the twenty other countries of the world. According to Census 2011, India has 104 million tribal population which constitutes 8.6 per cent of the total population of the country. There are total 461 recognised groups as tribes; estimated total unrecognised groups are 705. During independence, India was committed to the multifaceted equality, liberty and fraternity to all the people of India in general and the marginalised sections of the society, in particular. Constitution makers were also concerned with the protection of the tribes from exploitation of all kinds. After independence in the developmental policy programmes, many action plans have been formulated to bring them at par with the main stream without affecting their distinctive character of their identity. Directive Principles of the state policy enshrined in Article 38 of the Constitution requires the state to secure social order for promotion of the welfare of the people, Article 38(2) envisages welfare not only of individuals but also of community, residing in different areas and engaged in different occupations. At the international level also the importance of protecting and promoting the interests of the indigenous tribal and non-tribal people in all the countries have been realised by UNO and other agencies India always honoured these developments at the international level. In 1957, ILO adopted 107th Convention in this context, it was ratified by India. Broadly the convention exhorted the signatories' countries to take steps for the individual and community development of the marginalised people. States should take steps to assure their property rights and their individual or collective ownership over the land which they traditionally occupy. In 1994, UNO Working Group on indigenous population adopted a draft declaration on the rights of the indigenous people. This draft declaration has immense importance. It recognises the democratic rights of the indigenous people to protect and promote their distinct identities in the broader perspective of the countries to which they belong. The Declaration recognises the freedom of the indigenous individuals and people to be free from any kind of adverse discrimination, based in particular on their indigenous origin or identity. Article 3 of the Declaration asserts that indigenous people have the right of self determination. By virtue of that right they can freely determine their political status and freely pursue their economic, social and cultural development. Article 23 provides that indigenous people have the right to determine and develop priorities and strategies for exercising their right to development (for details see Gupta et al. 1998: 86). Since independence the government has made special provisions of reservation in services as well as in the elected bodies (Parliament and State Legislatures) for the uplittment of the marginalised sections of the society, particularly Scheduled Tribes. Union government as well as the state governments has formulated sub plans for the development of the tribal areas. Government has established single line agencies in the tribal areas to make the development activities effective. Government policy of non-involvement of the people in general in the formulation of the local plans implementing those plans resulted into the lopsided development of the tribals in the country. In the beginning governments policy of 'policy decision by the top and implementation by the officials' created the gap between 'the need and given' of the tribal people. Centralised planning system, lack of representative institutions at the grassroots level led to the denial of the rights of the indigenous people, to decide their socio-economic political system according to their own norms and traditions. Various studies conducted in different tribal areas of the country. Tribal development forced more from the outside than generated from within (D.B. Negi in Gupta et al. 1998: 369). Developmental interference harmed rather than helped the tribal people to preserve their cultural heritage as well as modernise its tradition. It is a fact that in this pursuit of economic and technological development within a framework controlled by the economic and political elite from local to the global level, the tribal people disposed off resources which were traditionally under their control. As a result of this they are being pauperised, marginalised and are the being progressively alienated from other segments of the society.

Tribal community and their habitats constitute very significant parts of backward people and regions of the country respectively. In the Indian context, a tribe is defined as a group with traditional territory, specific name, common language, strong kin relations, association with clan structure, tribal authority, and rigid inclination to religion and belief. Functional independence, homogeneity, primitive means of exploiting resources, economic backwardness, rich culture and tradition and least desire to change are some of the other characteristics those dominant among the tribes (Pant 2010: 13).

The aborigines in Indian language are known as *Adibasi* : *Adi* and *basi* standing for 'original' and 'habitant' respectively. Constitutionally these human groups Scheduled Tribes (ST) are known by different local names, such as *Anusuchit Jati, Vanjati, Vanvasi, Pahari,* and *Adimjati,* etc. According to Article 342 of the Indian Constitution, 'The scheduled tribes are the tribes or tribal communities, which may be notified by the President of India'.

The main characteristic features of the Indian tribes are: variation in size of the population, presence in all climatic zones, belong to all in four races-Negrito, Proto-Austroloid, Mongoloid and Caucasoid and use Indo-Aryan, Dravidian and Tibeto-Burman language (Pant 2010: 14)

DEMOGRAPHIC FEATURES OF INDIAN TRIBES (2011)

Scheduled Tribe Population and Decade Change by Residence: 2011

	Scheduled Tribe Population		
	Total	*Rural*	*Urban*
India	10,42,81,034	9,38,19,162	10,4,61,872
	Decadal Change 2001–2011		
India	23.7	21.3	49.7

Scheduled Tribe Population by Sex and Residence: Census 2011

	Scheduled Tribe Population		
	Total	*Rural*	*Urban*
India	5,24,09,823	4,71,26,341	52,83,482
	Decadal Change 2001–2011		
India	5,18,71,211	4,66,92,821	51,78,390

Sex Ratio among Scheduled Tribes by Residence: Census 2011

	Scheduled Tribe Population		
	Total	*Rural*	*Urban*
India	978	981	944
	Decadal Change 2001–2011		
India	990	991	980

Percentage of Scheduled Tribes to Total Population: 2001–2011

	Scheduled Tribe Population		
	Total	*Rural*	*Urban*
India	8.2	10.4	2.4
	Decadal Change 2001–2011		
India	8.6	11.3	2.8

Source: Census of India 2011, Tribal Profile at a Glance.

Features of the Indian Tribes

Over the last 20–25 years, international tribal community has been incessantly trying to draw the attention of the world's leading power blocks to save them from perennial miseries. Currently there are about 300 million indigenous people living in 70 countries. They have come together to seek help from the UNO to put an end to their poverty as well as to social discrimination against them. In response, UNO has taken some decisive steps. World Health Organization (WHO) has emphasised that indigenous people have higher rate of infant mortality, lower life expectancy and more case of chronic illness than the non-indigenous population in their home countries (Rath 2006: 15). Long before this international effort, India had already made attempts to improve the condition of its tribal populations consisting of 461 groups and non-recognised 705 groups, they constitute 8.6 per cent of the total population of the country, making for a total tribal population of 10,42,81,034 according to the Census 2011. Among them about 80 per cent live in the 'central belt' and across the states of Maharashtra, Madhya Pradesh, Chhattisgarh, Bihar, Jharkhand and Orissa, West Bengal and Tripura in east. Remaining 20 per cent live in the north-east states of Meghalaya, Mizoram, Nagaland, Arunachal Pradesh, Sikkim and in the Union Territories of Dadra and Nagar Haveli, Andaman and Nicobar and Lakshadweep. A few of them live in southern states of Kerala, Tamil Nadu and Karnataka. Andhra Pradesh has the largest tribal population among southern states of the India (Rath 2006: 16).

Tribals have mainly located in the forest areas of country through the ages. Since times immemorial, tribal communities have constituted an important segment of the Indian society. They are different from the mainstream population due to their living conditions. In the past, they were isolated from others segments of the Indian society. Their seclusion was largely attributed to their habitat, their tendency to restrict their interaction within their own groups, lack of interest on the part of colonial masters in their affairs, their insecurities from the outer world. Tough terrain, lack of infrastructure in the area is also responsible for the marginalised plight of the tribals in the country. Forest and tribals have had a symbiotic relationship through the ages.

Tribal people are characterised as isolated in ecology, demography, economic aspects, political organisation and other social behaviour from other ethnic groups of India. The concept of the tribe as a socio-cultural organisation is of great significant. It is needless to state that the habitat of the tribal communities is generally hilly, forest and other inaccessible tracts. In the past they remained isolated from others except having some economic interactions with neighbouring communities. Due to living in isolation in the natural surrounding they developed certain specific features, viz. typical cultural background, ecology, economy, language, identity and the political system of their own, etc. (Sinha 2001: 359).

Tribal religion in India seems to have a common feature that all being are endowed with a living spirit. Animal, plants, rivers, mountains are exception to this rule. Dead who have apparently left us are yet with us, and it is though remembrance of offerings that we have to renew our relationship with them on due occasions. Dead are again reborn as offsprings in the present generations. All these practices are similar to Hindu religion. In the forest where some of the more isolated communities live, a few trees are never touched or cut, for they represent the primal grove. Pipal tree is also considered sacred and abode of Basudeo, a Hindu god. It is never cut down (Thakur 1997: 17).

It is almost obvious that the tribal community in India is extremely backward and poverty-stricken (61.9% in rural areas and 35% in urban area) (GOI, Planning Commission 2013). Statistical Profile Report of Scheduled Tribes 2013 by GOI also pointed out that the tribal people have less accessibility to the basic human needs. These include: housing facility, sanitation, drinking water and health care in comparison to the others. Deprivation is also one of the major causes of their inability to exploit their potential. Their employment profile also reflect that they work in the retail and manufacturing sectors, and in service sector their share is less as compare to the Scheduled Castes.

Tribal communities continue in the pastoral of shifting cultivation stage of economy till today. Tribal economy is intimately connected with the forests. Forest regions are, generally, inhabited by the tribal communities who are lagging behind in the economic development as compare to the other communities in the country.

Agriculture sector in the tribal regions is under developed due to the tough terrain and poor technological as well as institutional development. Whereas the acidic soil certainly act as a constraint on increasing productivity by indigenous methods, inadequacy of irrigation facilities. Tribals are considered socio-economically weaker sections of the society as they suffered a lot at the hands of the local rulers, traders, colonial powers non-tribals and the like forces. They have attuned themselves to their ecological and geo-climatic conditions throughout the country. They belong to the various linguistic, social, cultural and ethnic groups and have attained various levels of socio-economic development. They have rightful claim over some special salient features which make them unique. Cultural identification or way of living is still strong among them.

In fact, prior to the independence, British government adopted a policy of isolation of the tribals. This policy kept them off from the main stream of the Indian life and culture. Though the preservation of the tribal culture was the idea behind this policy of isolation, this led to the development of a cleavage between the tribal and non-tribal communities (Sahu 2001: 1). Tribals have been the victims of colonial domination, illiteracy, ignorance, caste prejudice, poverty and isolation. When India was declared an independent state, the question of the socio-economic development in respect of the scheduled tribes came into being under Article 46 of the Indian Constitution, to prevent their exploitation by the other groups of the society. To tackle these problems, various committees appointed by the Constituent Assembly (CA). On the basis of the reports of these committees some special provisions have been incorporated in the Constitution of India for the welfare of the Scheduled Tribes. Government of India (GOI) initiated wide spread Tribal Development Programmes (TDP) effectively since Fifth Five Year Plan (1974–79) under the new name Tribal Sub-Plan (TSP) to improve their socio-economic condition, quality of life and asset accumulation (Fifth Five Year Plan). Long term objectives of the Tribal Sub-Plan approach were to narrow down the gap between the tribal and non-tribals. In brief, the approach envisaged tackling of tribal problems by categorising them under three identified areas and groups:

1. In regions of substantial tribal concentration, an area development approach is to be combined with the focus on the tribal population and their problems.
2. In smaller areas of dispersed tribal population, where the Scheduled Tribes live merged with the general population, a modified area approach on account of the truncated natured of the habitat.
3. Certain extremely backward and smaller tribal groups living generally in pre-agricultural level of the technology in inaccessible areas and facing the problem of their very survival would be treated as a special category both within the areas of tribal concentration and outside special group-oriented programmes would be formulated for them.

Three categories were brought under the Integrated Tribal Development Project (ITDP), Modified Area Development Approach (MADA) Pockets, and Primitive Tribe Projects respectively (Sahu 2001: 127–128).

Health is intimately linked to these essentials of living. Health status of India's tribal communities is in need of special attention. Being among the poorest and most marginalised groups in India, tribals experience is extreme levels of health deprivation. Tribal community lags behind the national average on several vital public health indicators, with women and children being the most vulnerable. The maternal health shows poorer nutritional status, higher levels of morbidity and mortality (212 per thousand), and lower utilisation of antenatal and post-natal services among tribes. Under five mortality rates among the rural tribal children is still high. It is double than the national under five mortality. Health problems prevalent in tribal areas include endemic infectious diseases like malaria, tuberculosis, and diarrhea, apart from malnutrition and anaemia (Swaminathan 2014: No. 209).

Nearly 75 per cent of India's tribal population defecates in the open and 33 per cent does not have access to a clean source of drinking water. Insanitary conditions, ignorance, lack of health education and poor access to health care facilities are the main factors responsible for the poor health of the tribals. Government has provided for the establishment of Primary Health Centres (PHCs) in tribal areas for every 20,000 and sub-centres for every 3,000, quality health care is not available to the majority of the tribal population. Though some traditional practices and superstitions persist, acceptance of modern medicine has increased in recent years, but access to good health care is the major issue. Levels of illiteracy are high, with 47 per cent in rural areas and 21.8 per cent in urban areas being unable to read and write. Most tribal groups are traditionally hunter-gatherers and not accustomed to agriculture. Their diet, therefore, are now severely limited to fruits and vegetables as well as good source of protein (Swaminathan 2014: Vol. 4).

Conclusion

India is one of the countries where twenty per cent of the total tribal population of the world resides. Indian tribes are heterogeneous sub-groups. Their distinct identities are results of the multifaceted diversities. Besides diversities tribal society of India has some common characteristics: less developed, culturally rich and strong passion to protect their distinct identity.

4

Indian Constitution and Scheduled Tribes

Constitution provides various safeguards for the promotion and protection of the interests of the Scheduled Tribes. Provisions contained in Articles 19, 46, 164, 244, 275, 330, 332, 334, 338, 339, 342 and 5th and 6th Schedules of the Indian Constitution are relevant in this regard. Government of India's responsibility in relation to the development of Scheduled Tribes and the Schedule Areas extends not only to the provision of Article 275 for their development but also to evolving policies and programmes for their rapid and harmonious development in consultation with and cooperation of the State Government (Biswas 2008: 334). Preamble of the Indian Constitution and the Directive Principles of the State Policy amply demonstrate term 'tribe' that state is committed to welfare of the people, pledged fully to raise the level of the standard of living, to improve public health, to promote the educational and economic interests of the weaker sections of the society. Tribe is nowhere clearly defined in the Constitution and in fact there is no perfect or fool proof definition anywhere. To the ordinary man the word suggests simple folk living in hills and forests with their 'exotic' culture, it signifies 'colourful' folks known for their dances, songs and folk medicines. Under the Constitution the President may specify by public notification through the Article 342 which shall for purposes of this constitution be deemed to be Scheduled Tribes in relation to that state or union territory as case maybe.

With the dawn of Independence and adoption of the Constitution of free India, responsibility for their welfare and development was placed on the popular government through the President and Governors of the state. In pursuance of the Directive Principles, special articles have been provided for the welfare of the Scheduled Castes and Scheduled Tribes. Most of them are common to both of these categories while a few exclusively meant for either of these. These Constitutional provisions may be divided into two groups underlying the following themes:

1. Protection
2. Development

The protective provisions provide them protection from the social and economic exploitation and injustice. Provisions relating to the development of the Scheduled Tribes are meant for providing them positive steps for their socio-economic development. Following is the summarised narration of these constitutional provisions.

Protective Provisions

Article 15(4): Promotion of Social, Economic and Educational Interests

Though Article 15 prohibits any discrimination on grounds of religion, race, caste, sex or place of birth but the Clause (4) of this Article provides an exception to this. It empowers the state to make any special provision for the advancement or socially and educationally backward classes of the citizens or for the Scheduled Castes and Scheduled Tribes. This provision is in accordance with the policy envisaged in Article 46 that the state should promote with special care educational and economic interests of the weaker sections of the people and protects them from social injustice.

Article 16(4): Reservation in Posts and Services and Article 19(5) – Safeguard of Tribal Interest in Property

While the right of free movement and residence throughout the territory of India and of acquisition and disposition of property are guaranteed to every citizen, special restrictions may be imposed by the State for the protection of the interests of the members of the Scheduled Tribes under Article 19(5).

Article 23: Prohibition of Trafficking in Human Beings and Forced Labour, etc.

It prohibits trafficking in human beings, beggars or forced labourers. This is a very important provision because the Scheduled Tribes being much vulnerable to the economic exploitation and prone to be victim of the economically sound class. In fact a substantial number of the tribal population in the country has been leading a miserable life as bonded labour.

Article 29: Cultural and Educational Rights

Article 29(2) is controlled by the Clause 4 of Article 15

Incorporated in the Constitution by the First Amendment Act 1951. This has brought Article 15 and 29 in line with Articles 16(4), 46 and 340 and made it constitutional for the state to reserve seats for the backward classes of the citizens, in public educational institutions. According to Article 29 a cultural or linguistic minority has a right to conserve its language or culture. This article provides protection to Scheduled Tribe communities to preserve their languages, dialects and cultures.

Article 46: Promotion of Educational and Economic Interests of Scheduled Castes, Scheduled Tribes and Other Weaker Sections

Article 164: Minister in-charge of Tribal Welfare in the State of Bihar, Orissa and Madhya Pradesh

This Article provides for a Minister in-charge of tribal welfare in the states of Bihar, Orissa and Madhya Pradesh. These states have substantial tribal populations and special provision of a Minister looking after tribal welfare. It is an evidence of the concern of the framers of the Constitution to safeguard the interests of the Scheduled Tribes.

Article 330, 332 and 334: Reservation in the Lok Sabha and the Vidhana Sabha's seat for Scheduled Tribes, Article 335: Describes Limits of the Reservation, Article 338: Special Officer

There shall be a special officer for the Scheduled Castes and Scheduled Tribes to be appointed by the President of India. It shall be the duty of the special officer to investigate all the matters relating to the safeguards provided for the Scheduled Castes and Scheduled Tribes under the Constitution. He shall report to the President upon the working of these safeguards at such intervals as the President may direct. The President shall call all such reports to be laid before each house of the Parliament. Such an officer has been designated as commissioner for the Scheduled Castes and Scheduled Tribes. By virtue of the Constitutional 65th Amendment Act, 1990, the post of the 'Special Officer' has been substituted by the National Commission for Scheduled Castes and Scheduled Tribes. Commission shall consist of a chairperson, vice-chairperson and five other members to be appointed by the President of India.

Article 275 and 339: Provision meant for the Economic Development

Provisions relating to economic development of Scheduled Tribes are mainly contained in Articles 275 and 339. Article 275 of the Constitution provides for the assistance of the states for the implementation of the provisions of the Constitution. Article 339 lays down that the 'executive' power of the Union Government extends to the giving of directions to a state as to drawing up and execution of schemes specified in the direction to be essential for the welfare of the Scheduled Tribes in the state. Tribal sub-plans are also part of the strategy to implement the provisions of the Constitution for the tribals on pan India level.

Scheduled Areas

Scheduled areas are the areas which are decided by the President of India in the consultation with the governor of the respective states. President can also increase or decrease the area, alter the boundary of Scheduled area with the consultation of the governor. Such area remains separate because the people of the area, having totally different culture, tradition, being backward economically they need special attention. Scheduled Tribes live in contiguous areas unlike other communities. It is, therefore, much simpler to have an area approach for the development activities as well as regulatory provisions to protect their interests. In order to protect the interests of Scheduled Tribes with regard to land and other social issues, various provisions have been enshrined in the Fifth Schedule and the Sixth Schedule of the Constitution. Article 244(1) provides the provisions of the Fifth Schedule shall apply to the administration and control of the Scheduled Areas and Scheduled Tribes in any state other than the states of Assam, Meghalaya, Tripura and Mizoram. These councils have wide ranging legislative, judicial and executive powers in the Constitution of India.

Fifth Scheduled Areas

The criteria for declaring any area as a 'Scheduled Area' under the Fifth Schedule are:

- Preponderance of tribal population,
- compactness and reasonable size of the area,
- a viable administrative entity such as a district, block or *taluk*,
- economic backwardness of the area as compared to the neighbouring areas.

The specification of scheduled areas in relation to a state is by a notified order of the President, after consultation with the state government concerned. The same applies in the case of any alteration, increase, decrease, incorporation of new areas, or rescinding any orders relating to 'Scheduled Areas' (Annual Report 2012–13: 39).

Under the Presidential order certain tribal areas have been declared as scheduled areas in the state of Andhra Pradesh, Bihar, Gujarat, Madhya Pradesh, Maharashtra, Orissa, Rajasthan and Himachal Pradesh. The main features of the Fifth Schedule are the (i) Special legislative powers of the Governor, (ii) Governor's Report to the President, and (iii) Constitution of a Tribal Advisory Council.

Sixth Schedule

Sixth Schedule applies to the tribal areas within the States of Assam, Meghalaya, Mizoram and Tripura. Among the main features of the tribal areas are: (i) their full autonomy in respect of the matters falling within their jurisdiction. In other words these areas may be described as 'states within a state', (ii) power of self management to the tribals through autonomous district and autonomous regions, and (iii) autonomy of these areas to such an extent that the writ of the Parliament or the state legislature do not see automatically unless the Acts in the whole or part are specifically extended to the tribal areas by notification of the Governor.

Special Provisions with Respect to Tribal Areas and Hill Areas of Nagaland, Assam and Manipur

Article 371(A) (Nagaland)

As per provisions of this Article, no act of the Parliament in respect of the (i) religious or social practices of Nagas, (ii) Naga customary laws and procedures, (iii) administration of civil and criminal justice involving decisions according to Naga Customary Law, and (iv) ownership and transfer of land and its resources, shall not apply to the state of Nagaland unless allowed by a special resolution of the Nagaland Assembly.

Article 371(B) (Assam)

The President may provide for the Constitution and function of a committee of the legislative assembly of the state consisting of members of that assembly elected from the tribal areas as specified in the Sixth Schedule and such other members of that assembly as may be specified in the order. Committee has been provided to look after the interests of the tribal areas at the state level.

Article 371(C) (Manipur)

Article 371(C) provides for the Constitution and functions of a committee through a Presidential order. Committee shall consist of the members of the legislative assembly elected from hill areas of the state. Governor has been required to submit an annual report to the President regarding the administration of the Hill Areas in the state of Manipur.

Union executive has been empowered to issue directions to the state as to the administration of the said areas.

Constitution of India contains number of important provisions relating to the tribal issues. These include statutory recognition of the tribal communities; their proportionate representation in the legislatures, right to have own language for education and other purposes.

Jawaharlal Nehru's philosophy and vision shaped the tribal policy in the 1950s, particularly in North-East. Nehru's views quoted in K.S. Singh (1985: 250), 'I am alarmed when I see not only in this country but in other countries too how anxious people are to shape others according to their own images or likeness, and to impose on them their particular way of living. In certain respects I am quite certain this is better. Therefore, it is grossly presumptuous on our part to approach them with an air of superiority or to tell them what to do or not to do. There is no point in trying to make them a second rate copy of ourselves'. For the next 45 years rural India with tribal intersection was not able to attain the status of a political community which could have enjoyed the status of 'a community that was responsible to write its own destiny'. In this field 73rd Amendment is the landmark step which became the foundation for the PESA Act 1996.

PESA Act, 1996

To meet the impediments faced in the tribal areas, on the basis of 73rd Amendment Panchayats Extension to Scheduled Areas Act (PESA Act, 1996) is a law enacted by the Government of India (GOI). Act's basic purpose was to meet the gaps those were the outcomes of the centralised planning and execution of the development programmes by the officials. Natives as the main stake holders had no role in the governance except electing the representative for the national Parliament and state legislature. PESA is an act to ensure self-governance in the tribal areas under Schedule V of the Indian Constitution. Tribal society from the times immemorial evolved their own systems based on the requirements, PESA provides space to modernise those practices by adopting the new practices and accommodating them within the Indian Constitution. In this act, vast powers have been given to the Gram Sabha (GS) and the three tier Panchayati Raj Institutions (PRIs), Gram Sabha as an institution of direct democracy empowered to permit the outsiders to use or not to use the land and other natural resources in the area. It is also authorised to decide the issues related to the Minor Forest Products (MFP) which further strengthened by the Forest Rights Act 2006 (FRA). In deciding the development plans, GS and PRIs have been given special rights. In tribal areas further reservation has been given to the women and Schedule Castes in the PRIs. After PESA at the village level Gram Sabha and its executive body Panchayat legally laced with enormous powers to manage the community and control its resources. Different sources governmental reports (Statistical Profile Report 2013) and research project by the NGOs and researchers at the universities level indicate after enactment of PESA the system in tribal society has not improved much. Still the institutions of the Gram Sabha and PRIs are not effective. People are not aware about their rights given in the Act. Government and the non tribal entrepreneurs encroach their rights. Big corporate houses misuse their lands and natural resources after the liberalisation of Indian economy in 1991. Government policy of Liberalisation, Privatisation and Globalisation (LPG) kept little space for the protection of the rights of the tribals who are still on the backfoot of development. In the initial stages when there were no statutory provisions like PESA, FRA and RTI, tribals and their resources were in great danger. Today when these Acts are in force, to some extent, the tribals are also conscious about their situation. NGOs and civil society started showing their interest in the tribes with the corporate intervention in the tribal areas. It is a matter of special concern to protect the tribal society from the menace of the corporate world. In case of Maharashtra, the irrigation department procured tribal land for irrigation project on meagre rates. Seven villages in Dharma *tehsil* of Maharashtra raised their voice against the project and demanded work to be stopped till their demands met. Panchayat members said that the work started without taking the Gram Sabha's consent. This indicates the violation of provisions of the PESA Act 1996 which provides the status of legislature to Gram Sabha (Panchayati Raj update, March 2012). In other states also Orissa, Madhya Pradesh, West Bengal, Bihar and Himachal Pradesh agitations against the corporate by the masses through civil society and NGOs have become common feature. In Himachal some of the retired bureaucrats, doctors who belong to the tribal area initiated drive to aware the tribal regarding corporate and their rights under PESA to decide the avenues of development in their area. Ground reality reflects that none of the states having tribal areas under Schedule V have effective institution of the Gram Sabha at the village level till now. Reasons for such conditions are ignorance, apathetic attitude of the state governments, lack of will on the part of the bureaucracy and political leadership's conception is that emergence of strong leaders at the local level may be challenge to the state leadership.

In tribal societies also there are inequities based on caste and class which were prevalent during the colonial period. The warrior and aristocrat class enjoy better status while tenants were considered to be low in status. After the independence in most of the tribal pockets the system became rigid and gradually caste evolved in these societies and the power structure formal or informal controlled by the elite section of the society.

Conclusion

In Indian Constitution special efforts were made in the form of fundamental rights, directive principles and affirmative actions to protect the tribals. Government policies and planning in the last seventy years have not been able to achieve the desired results. 73rd Amendment and on its lines PESA Act 1996 is a step to promote democracy and recognition of the right of indigenous people to manage their affairs according to their age old practices. After more than twenty years of the enactment of the PESA Act it is imperative to review the developments in the tribal society which is facing the intrusion of corporate in their domain.

5

Major Tribes in India

State Wise Status

There are 715 Scheduled Tribes notified under Article 342 of the Constitution of India, spread over different states and Union Territories of the country. Demographic statistics of Tribes in India form the largest proportion of the total population of Lakshadweep and Mizoram followed by Nagaland and Meghalaya. Madhya Pradesh has the largest number of Scheduled Tribes, followed by Bihar. Bastar district of Chhattisgarh consists of largest number of Scheduled Tribes. There are no Scheduled Tribes in Punjab, Delhi, Chandigarh, Pondicherry, Haryana and Jammu and Kashmir.

Different Classifications of the Tribes

Indian tribes can be classified on the bases of the diverse variables. Tribes are common in all parts of the country. Vast size of the country and multiple diversities have impact on the tribal society of India. Indian tribes may be classified on the basis of their: (i) territorial distribution, (ii) linguistic affiliation, (iii) physical and racial characteristics, (iv) occupation or economy, and (v) religious beliefs.

Geographical Classification

1. *North and North-eastern Zone:* Northern and North-eastern zone consists of the sub-Himalayan region and the mountain valleys of the eastern frontiers of India. The tribal people of Assam, Manipur and Tripura may be included in the eastern part of this geographical zone, in north the tribals of eastern Kashmir, eastern Punjab, Himachal Pradesh and northern Uttar Pradesh are included.
2. *Central or the Middle Zone:* This zone consists of plateaus and mountainous belt between the Indo-Gangetic plain to the North and

roughly the Krishna River to the South and this is separated from the North-eastern zone by the gap between the Garo hills and the Rajmahal hills. In this zone tribal people in Madhya Pradesh with extensions in Uttar Pradesh, Madhya Bharat, southern Rajasthan, northern Maharashtra, Bihar and Orissa.

3. *Southern Zone:* This zone consists of that part of southern India which falls south of the river Krishna stretching from Wynaad to Cape Comorin. Andhra Pradesh, Karnataka, Coorg, Travancore, Cochin, Tamil Nadu, etc. are included in this zone.

Linguistic Classification

At present people of India may be divided into four speech families, viz. the Indo-European (Aryan), the Dravidian, the Austric (Kolar Munda) and the Tibeto-Chinese (Sino-Tibetan). Most of the scholars, therefore, are of the view that the tribal people of India may be classified chiefly into three speech families: (1) Dravidian, (2) Austric, and (3) Tibeto-Chinese.

The tribal people speaking the language falling under Dravidian speech family inhabit the middle and southern India. Most developed languages of Dravidian family are Tamil, Telugu, Kannada and Malayalam. Gonds occupy the chief place among the tribal speeches derived from Dravidian family and it is spoken widely by the Gond tribals who are scattered from Madhya Pradesh to Andhra Pradesh. The speeches of Toda, Chenchu, Paliya, Chenchu, Irula and Kadar are also included in the Dravidian family.

The Austric family of speeches is also known as Munda speech family. Speeches of this family are spoken mainly by the tribals of Chotanagpur area but these are also in vogue, to a lesser extent, in some parts of Madhya Pradesh, Orissa, West Bengal, Madaras and Terai region of Himalayas stretching from Bihar to Shimla hills.

Tibeto-Chinese speeches are spoken most by the tribals of Mongol racial stock. This family is divided into two branches: (i) Tibeto-Burman, and (ii) Siamess-Chinese. The tribals of Assam, Meghalaya and other parts of the North-east India speak one or the other speeches of this area.

Racial Classification

The complexity of the problem of classifying the tribal people of India on the basis of racial affinities that fixing the racial origins or affinities of the tribal communities of India is one of the most complicated tasks those have had to be faced by the Indian anthropologists.

The first scientific racial classification of India was attempted by Sir Herbert Hope Risely. He published his findings in 1915 in the book 'The

People of India'. He classifies the entire Indian population into seven racial types: (i) Turko-Iranian, (ii) Indo-Aryan, (iii) Scytho-Dravidian, (iv) Aryo-Dravidian, (v) Mongolo-Dravidian, (vi) Mongoloid, (vii) Dravidian.

These seven types may be reduced to three basic types, viz. the Dravidian, Mongolian and Indo-Aryan. Significantly, he gave no separate classificatory scheme for the 'aboriginals' of India.

Economic Classification

Tribal economy is normally considered to be backward based on the agriculture (based on the traditional methods) hunting, rearing livestock and doing petty jobs near to their habitats. On the basis of their economic activities the tribals can be classified as: (i) those tribes who live by hunting in forests earn their livelihood through collection of edible roots and fruits, hunting and fishing. This class of the tribes is found mostly in southern India, (ii) a vast chunk of Indian tribes is engaged in shifting cultivation hilly or mountainous tracts of north-eastern and central India. Almost all the tribes of Assam, Meghalaya, Arunachal Pradesh, Mizoram, Manipur and Tripura produce their crops through this mode of cultivation, (iii) some of the Indian tribes earn their livelihood through cottage industries, (iv) pastoral tribes are few in number but Toda of Nilgiri hills, Gaddi and Bakarwal of Himachal Pradesh, Nageshia of Madhya Pradesh, Maldhan of Gujarat and some other tribes of northern and southern India are notable examples of this class of tribes, (v) another class of tribes earn their livelihood by performing dances, acrobatics, snake charming, etc. and hence they may be termed as 'folk artist'.

Classification Based on Religious Beliefs

Major religions of India have variably influenced various tribal religious practices and only those tribal communities still maintain their native religious beliefs with purity who are leading almost isolated social existence in the dense forests. On the basis of the latest census data, tribes may be classified into followers of following religions: (i) Hinduism (ii) Christianity (iii) Buddhism (iv) Islam (v) Jainism (vi) Other religions.

Among the above mentioned religions, the influence of Hindu religion on the tribes is tremendous and almost ninety per cent tribals follow Hindu religion in one form or the other. Those who have embraced Christianity are also quite considerable in number and about six per cent are under the 'shadow of the cross' but those following Buddhism, Islam or Jainism are negligible in number. One important point which is to be kept in mind in this context is that even those tribes who have embraced any of the above mentioned major religions have not necessarily shed their local tribal beliefs and rituals and many of them are found to be practicing their traditional faith along with their acquired faith. Their religious beliefs cannot be compartmentalised. They are innocent people who adopt the practices from the beginning according to their utility and relevance in their life.

State Wise Tribal Profile

After Independence with the reorganisation of the states tribal can also be classified on the basis of political units 'state wise'. North-east states come under the Schedule VI of the Indian Constitution, and under the Schedule V of the Constitution rest of the states those have tribal population come within the purview of this Schedule.

Madhya Pradesh Tribes

Madhya Pradesh is not only one of the largest states in India, but also has the maximum tribal population of the country. State is located in the centre of the Indian Union; its borders are adjoining the tribal regions of bordering states. Geographically, the state extends more than 1,000 kilometres from north to south and east to west. Vast area of the state and the sparseness of the population in the tribal regions make it more difficult and expensive to provide the same level of the facilities and services as in other states of the country. Therefore, in spite of its large size and great potential in the natural resources, Madhya Pradesh remains one of the most backward states of the Indian Union.

State has been divided into five cultural zones. Western region having highest concentration of the tribal population, predominantly inhabited by the Bhil and Bhilala tribals in Jhabua, Dhar, West Nimar, East Nimar and Ratlam districts. The central region is predominantly inhabited by Gonds, Korkus and Baigas. The major concentration of the tribal population is in Mandla, Balaght, Chhindwara and Seoni districts. The north-eastern region is predominantly inhabited by the Gonds. Kol is another backward tribe inhabiting this region. Heavy concentration of the tribal population is in Shahdol and Sidhi districts. The eastern region is rich in forest and mineral resources. Predominant, population is that of Oraons, Gonds, Kanwar and Pahari-Korwas tribes. The southern region of the state is popularly known as Maria-Muria track, with a sizeable population of Gonds, Halbas, Bhatras and Dorlas (Nanaria and Vaishnavi 1998: 85).

Madhya Pradesh is a large state with vast physical and ethnic diversity. It has been the home of several primitive tribes of India and has the largest tribal population in the country. According to Census 2011, the tribal population of the state is about 15.31 million out of 72.62 million which accounts 21.10 per cent of the total state population. Major tribes of the state are Abujhmarhia, Baiga, Bhil, Birhor, Bhatra, Bharia, Gond, Kamar, Pando, Korba, Pando, Kol, Oraon and Sahareiya, etc. and are distributed in different tribal zones. Majority of the tribes inhabitants of or around the dense forest areas and their entire life is wholly or partially dependent upon the forest resources.

Madhya Pradesh Government has declared seven most primitive tribes. They are Abujhmarhias, Baiga, Bharias, Birhors, Hill Korbas, Kamars and Sahariyas. At the state level, the Department of Tribal Development is headed by the cabinet rank minister under whom a State Minister of Tribal Development is also functioning. At the secretariat level the activities of the department is looked after by a senior IAS officer in the rank of a Principal Secretary. The policy matters are dealt at this level. There is also a separate Directorate of the Tribal Development headed by the Commissioner Tribal Development. It implements the development programmes in the tribal areas of the state. State also has a separate directorate for the tribal development. Its functions are planning and monitoring of the developmental programmes (Joshi 1998: 89).

MP tribes have some common social, economic and political features. All the tribal communities are endogamous groups, patriarchal, patrilineal societies. From the primitive shifting agro practices they switched over to the settled agricultural economy. With the growing boom of corporate they also work as daily wagers in the corporate sector. Corporate activities affected their community life also. They live in the small villages. Informal power structures, their customary governing practices are still followed. Besides the implementation of the PESA Act 1996, there is overlapping in the functions of the formal power and informal power structures. Traditional institutions, roles and cultural practices have pre-dominant role in the tribal life.

Odisha Tribes

Number of the tribal people in India is perhaps the largest in the world, after Africa. Half of India's tribal population is concentrated in the relatively underdeveloped states: Bihar, Odisha and Madhya Pradesh. According to the Census 2011, as much as 22.1 per cent of the total population of the state of Odisha belongs to the Scheduled Tribes, among whom about sixty different, ethno-culturally separate communities are recognised. There are districts like Mayurbleny, Koraput, Sundergarh, Keoughar and Phulbani, where the tribal population ranges from 40 to 60 per cent of the total population. Concentration of the tribal people varies widely in the remaining districts, ranging from the lowest three per cent in Cuttack district to the highest 28 per cent in Sambalpur district (Kumar 1994: 190).

State of the Odisha hosts more than 9.7 per cent of the total tribal population of the country. It consists of 62 communities. About 45 per cent of the total area in the state is declared as Scheduled Area under the Fifth Schedule of the Constitution. Forest area in the state is 9,963.30 sq km constituting 38 per cent of the total area of the state. The districts of Sundergarh, Mayurbhanj, Koraput and Raygada, five entire subdivisions, viz., Keoujhar, Sadar, Champua, Phulbani, Balliguda and Kuchinda, one full tehsil, i.e. Udaigiri, part of Suruda tehsil and five Community Development Blocks, namely, Nilagiri, Thuamul, Lanjiagarh, Gumma and Kashipur comprise the Scheduled Areas in Odisha and as many as 22 tribal dialects are spoken. Predominant tribal people are the Khond, Saura and the Bhuiya, Gond, Santal, Oraon and the Munda. In addition to the communities like Juang, Bhuiya, Dongria and Kutia Khonds and Langia Saora are included in the list of primitive tribes (Pathy 2004: 231).

Out of the total 62 tribal communities in Odisha 12 communities declared as primitive tribes. Census 2011 shows that among the ST population 4.77 per cent of the total workers work in the household industry 33.35 per cent are cultivators and 46.85 per cent are agricultural labourers. The tribals, thus, mostly work in the agriculture sector. Under Article 244 (Fifth Schedule) Odisha is covered under the 'Scheduled Area'. In Odisha, Oriya is the predominant language spoken by more than 80 per cent of the population. It is the official language of the state. Literacy level is low among the tribals, 16 out of 30 districts are below the state average literacy. The tribal male literacy rate is 63.70 per cent and female is 41.20 per cent.

Sub-culture of the tribal groups varies from one tribe to the other. It can be generalised to some extent. Tribal society mainly dependents for its living on the natural resources of the forests. There is community orientation among the tribals. Land usually communally owned, communal hunting, gathering, pastorals are significant features of the tribals. Development, exposure, globalisation, etc. modern conditions of mining, forestry, migration, interventions have affected their areas and culture (Mishra 2006: 62–65). Located on India's east coast, Odisha despite its generous endowment of mineral wealth, forest, lakes, rivers, a long coastline and a rich and ancient history with vast untapped potential for both cultural and eco-tourism, has been suffering from 'extreme poverty'. Due to the 'central neglect', unequal allocation of the resources in economic sphere and 'administrative apathy' the state has been denied of a 'fair deal' in the provincial autonomy and central subsidies right from the colonial period. This consequently coloured the Oriyas 'self-image' as backward and marginal group in India's polity, democracy and the discourse of the development (Sahoo 2007: 392).

Bihar Tribes

Bihar occupies important place in the 'Tribal India'. In Chotanagpur plateau it contains a tribal belt covering some of the largest tribes of the country such as the Oraon, Munda, Ho, Santhals, etc. The tribal population of the Bihar is around nine million (Census 2011) which comes about 10.06 per cent of the total population of the state. Although Bihar is placed at the 12th position in terms of the ranking of the states by schedule tribe percentage but in term of absolute number it is behind only Madhya Pradesh and Odisha. Of the total Scheduled Tribe population of the country, the tribals living in Bihar constitute about one fifth segment of the total population. Most of these tribes inhabit Hazaribagh, Dhanbad, Singhbhum, Palamu and Santhal Pargana. Besides these, considerable tribal population is found also in Sahasa, Bhabhua, Bhagalpur, Mungher, Purnia and Champaran. Among the main and relatively known tribes come Munda, Oraon, Ho, Santhal, Kharia, Pahariya and Birhor (Hasnain 2011: 151).

Like the other tribals of India, Bihar is not a monolith. It is the home of heterogeneous tribes with different linguistic and racial affiliations, living at different levels of the economic development. Birhor and hill Kharia are still food gatherer hunters while the tribes like Asur, Korwa and Mal Pahariya practice shifting cultivation. The larger tribes like Munda, Oraon, Ho, Santhal, etc. have transformed the process of Hinduisation and spread of Christianity presents important dimensions of their religious affiliation. In the demographic terms, the large tribes show normal, consistent growth of the population, among the relatively small tribes, tribal population either is stagnant or they are afflicted by depopulation (Hasnain 2011: 152). Bhiror is one of them. In the tribes like Santhal, development is visible. Their economy is agro economy. They also work as labourers. Due to their hard work and entrepreneurship they explored many economic activities for them in the liberal economic set up of today. In Bihar tribes' village system, customary panchayats are very common. Mostly tribal issues are settled in the purview of the tribal panchayats. Patriarchy and monogamy is common among the tribes. In case of adultery, divorce practice is followed. Women manage the indoor work along with partial agriculture activities.

National Movement and Tribal Contribution

The tribal people, by and large, remained isolated and backward, and their participation in the national politics, unlike that of the Harijans, was inconsiderable. They were almost the last one of the Indian communities to be politicised.

India is a country with large population of tribes after Africa. Indian tribes are not homogenous segment of the society. Tribals in different parts of the country differ from each other. Geography, their distance from the main stream and ethnic practices, all these factors contribute to the variations in their set ups in different parts of the country. Some of the tribals are comparatively developed to those who are still on the primitive stages of the development. Santhal tribes of Bihar and Himachal tribes are good examples of the developed tribes. Distinct features of the sub-tribal groups are composite culture and they are endogamous in nature. They try to maintain their solidarity. On the development scale over all India tribes are less developed. They need special care being one of the neglected segments of the society for centuries.

Conclusion

Tribes constitute a small but important segment of Himachal society. These are descendants of the earliest inhabitants of the sub-continent. They contributed to the variety and riches of cultural forms in the country. Over the centuries they have preserved a distinctive style of life; in terms of quality life and cultural ethos. There are significant differences among the tribes themselves in different parts of the country. Tribal groups represent different levels of socio-economic development. They differ greatly in their numbers and complexity of social organisation and there are variation in their customs and institutions.

6

Historiography of Himachal Tribes

Himachal is a part of the western Himalayas. It has unique demography and topography. On the one side it has plain terrain and on the other side it has its boundaries with Tibet the toughest terrain of the world. Demographically, people of the plains have culture affinity with Punjab and Haryana. Upper areas of the state have their own local cultural practices which they follow religiously. Himachal tribes have their own distinctions. Within the Himachal tribes they have sub-groups and follow heterogeneous practices in three tribal regions. Total population of Himachal Pradesh according to Census 2011 is 68,64,602 with a density of 123 persons per sq km. The highest density is in Hamirpur district which is 407 persons per sq km and the lowest is 2 persons per sq km in Lahaul Spiti (tribal area) district. About 89 per cent of the population lives in rural areas out of that 5.7 per cent is tribal population. According to Census 2011, number of the females per thousand males was total 974. Total Scheduled Caste population of Himachal is 17,29,252 which is 25.19 per cent of the total population of the state. Scheduled Tribe population of Himachal is 3,92,126 which is 5.7 per cent of the total population of the state (Census of India 2011). According to the World Bank Report (2015) joint press release on 28 January 2015 by the title 'Scaling the Heights: Social Inclusion and Sustainable Development in Himachal Pradesh' over the years Himachal Pradesh has made great strides in reducing extreme poverty and has emerged one of the states with the best of human developments outcomes in India … . Their support for the current growth is conditional on the extent to which the state's social and environmental heritage will be protected. World Banks Report suggests the state has performed well in the short term. State got the status of statehood on 26 January 1971.

Himachal folk is simple in living and thinking. Pre-dominantly it is a rural state. 89 per cent population here resides in the villages. People live in the village consisting of few hamlets dotted over the fields. Villages are found wherever an area of arable land exists, sufficient to support a few families. Villages are generally situated in the valleys, on terraces, or on spur tops. Village is the most important unit of the social economic and political system in Himachal Pradesh. It is an age old institution which served as the basic unit of the community life. People have strong bonding as community. They honour the common decisions taken by the elders of the village. Their disputes related to the matrimony, land are normally settled at the village level. They do not believe in litigation. Traditional institutions and roles are still dominant in the village life. Caste, class, patriarchy and joint family system, are the most significant features of the society. Land lord class which normally belongs to the upper castes controls the power system at all the levels. Masses do not have regrets with the traditional system which is based on caste based stratification and class variable has also important role in the system. They follow the traditional roles without questioning the persisting practices of behaviour in the democratic India. Village society is a close knit society ever willing to cooperate with their fellow villagers and share their problems. Fairs and festivals are the important part of the village life. Festivals are the expression of the culture where people by following the community norms express their commitment to their society. On these occasions, people meet each other and share festivity. With the passage of time these fairs also introduced them to the mainstream life. People from different parts of the country reach here and join the masses. Business class comes here for business purposes and big brand names also come for the marketing of their products. Good examples of fairs are Dusshera in Kullu, Shivratri in Mandi, Lavi in Rampur, Nalwar in Bilaspur and Sunder Nagar. People from the adjoining rural and tribal areas come in the fairs.

Agriculture is the main occupation of people of the state. About 70 per cent of the employed workers are engaged in agricultural sector. Agriculture is even now be set with the disadvantage of small holdings. Only 61 per cent of the total reporting area is available for the cultivation. But the major hindrance is that there is hardly any scope for mechanised farming due to the preponderance of small holdings and terraced fields. Against all these odds, the farmers of Himachal Pradesh are constantly endeavouring to fully exploit the agricultural potential of the state to increase food production and to supplement their income by producing quality crops. Horticulture in the upper reaches and mid hills is a major source of income. Fruit growing has a distinct advantage over cultivation of cereals or other cash crops in Himachal Pradesh because of typical agro-climatic conditions suitable for growing a large variety of fruits. Due to climatic variation, climate is also suitable for floriculture. Main aim of the development of floriculture is to develop commercial floriculture as a supplementary economic pursuit in orchards besides beautification of the important places through flower cultivation, ornamental gardening and landscaping. In all the tribal pockets of Himachal, like the other parts of the state, economic ventures and social institutions are almost same. Himachal tribals are gradually following the mainstream practices in day-to-day life style. Hinduisation of Himachal tribes is reflected in their day-to-day life. Their marriages are solemnised with the practices followed by Hindus. Dowry observing the fasts are also followed by the tribal women. Besides this trend, the tribal sub-groups being cultural identities try to maintain their distinct identities. Younger generation is also conscious about their cultural identity they prefer matrimonial alliances within their own tribal group. Cause maybe they do not want to lose the benefit of reservation.

Himachal Pradesh has good scope for the hydro power. It is extremely rich in its hydro power resources, having about twenty 25 per cent of the national potential in this respect. It has been estimated that about 27,436 MW of hydro power can be generated in the state by the construction of various hydro projects on the five perennial river basins notwithstanding their being major, medium or small. Out of total hydro potential of the state, 6,400 MW has been harnessed so far, out of which only seven per cent is under the control of Himachal Pradesh Government while the rest being exploited by the Central government or corporate houses. State government has been accorded the highest priority for its development, since hydro power generation can meet the growing need of power for the industry, agriculture and rural electrification. It is also biggest source of the income to the state as it provides electricity to the other states also (hydroelectric power in Himachal Pradesh-SJVN Ltd.). Industrialisation is a recent phenomenon in the state. It attained momentum after getting statehood in 1971. With a view to offset the topographical disadvantage and boost industrial development special incentives/packages were given to this hilly state for creating quality industrial infrastructure and motivating entrepreneurs to invest in the state, in order to create more employment opportunities and gear up the economy of the state. Share of industries in the Gross State Domestic Product is approximately 16 per cent. Tribal area is mainly involved in hydro power generation. All the five rivers either originate in the tribal pockets or the tribal areas are on the banks of these rivers. The growth of hydro economy has direct effect on the age old institutions and culture of the tribal society.

Handicrafts and Handloom industries have a huge potential in the state. In order to fully tap this potential, the state government is availing the Central Assistance available for promotion of these activities in the form of centrally sponsored schemes such as Integrated Handloom Development Scheme (IHDS), Handloom Weavers Comprehensive Welfare Scheme, Health Insurance Scheme and Mahatma Gandhi Bunkar Bima Yojana and marketing, export promotion and revival, reform and restructuring package for handloom sector which are primarily targeted to benefit handloom weavers. Tribal areas of Himachal experience long winters and for almost six months it is snow covered. People are confined to their houses. During long winters they engage themselves in the handicraft and handloom work. Cottage industry in the form of looms is very common among the Himachal tribes. Himachal tribal handicrafts and handlooms (shawls, socks and caps) are the most attractive features of the fairs and festivals within the state and outside. Looms and handicrafts substantiate their economy.

The State Gross Domestic Product (SGDP) at factor cost was 2016–17 is estimated 6.3 per cent and per capita income 1,58,462 in 2016–17 crore as against 1,13,355 crore in 2015–16 registering a growth of 6.3 per cent during the year. Agriculture sector contributed 13 per cent of the total GSDP, industry 43 per cent and service sector 42 per cent according to Economic Survey of Himachal 2017–18.

Rural Himachal and Power Structures after Independence

After the integration of the erstwhile states, arrangements to organise village panchayats and to equip them with necessary power and authority were made. Himachal Pradesh Panchayati Raj Act, 1952 came into force in 1953. As a result, legally constituted panchayats were established in 1954. Elections to these bodies were held in 1954, 58 and 62, with a term for three years for each panchayat (Mamgain 1971: 286). PRIs were equipped with some legal powers related to the development functions. But in practice they were powerless. No effort was made to give concrete shape to the local bodies by the national and state governments. This system was in force until the HP Panchayati Raj Act 1968 was passed. Under this Act, several panchayats were organised in the tribal area, although they were not financially strong. Financial decentralisation and resource mobilisation by the panchayats was not possible at that juncture. Status of the panchayats in the tribal areas was similar to the other parts of the country till the 73rd Amendment was passed by the Parliament. Panchayats were nominal institutions. Informal power structures (institution of the Devta, Chauras and representatives of the rajas normally acceptable person to the villagers) enjoyed the power and were responsible for the management of the village as a unit. After independence, due to seclusion and geo-climatic conditions, local administration was under the Deputy Commissioner in Kinnaur and Lahaul Spiti districts and Pangi in Chamba under the resident Commissioner in Pangi of district Chamba. They carried out regulatory and development assignments with much delegated administrative and financial powers. These arrangements were based on the centralised model of the development. People's participation had little scope. Bureaucracy was all pervasive. In such a milieu 73rd Amendment of the Indian Constitution is a watershed development in the field of rural local government. Through this Amendment, after 45 years of the independence, steps have taken to pave the way for real democracy, by recognising the right of the masses to participate in governance, directly and indirectly at the grassroots level. In case of the Scheduled Areas, where most of the people reside in tough terrains, they are far behind on the scale of the development as compared to the general masses. Dreze in Rath (2006) argued 'a terrible injustice has been done to tribal people in India. Repairing this injustice requires a better understanding of their societies, a more enlightened approach towards the tribal development, last but not least, a broad based political awakening among tribal communities themselves'. It is urgent to construct such structures as PRIs to ensure the process of the democratisation as well as to protect and promote the rich culture of these societies. Keeping in mind this perspective with regard to the Fifth Scheduled Areas, under Article 243(M) of the Constitution of India, on the recommendations of Duleep Singh Bhuria Committee, the provision of the Panchayati Raj Extension to the Scheduled Area was enacted by Parliament in 1996 (Hazra 2010: 29–38). PESA Act, 1996 is one the most progressive legislations for tribal regions for self-government and traditional rights of tribal communities over their natural resources.

In Himachal Pradesh the tribal areas have been the most secluded, remote, in accessible and comprise cold deserts, rugged and difficult terrain and the dreaded hill tracts (Thakur 1998: 123). Himachal tribal society, besides the fact it is a small segment of the Indian tribes, has distinct identity and enjoy better status in comparison to their tribal brother and sisters in other parts of the country. Tribal belt of Himachal Pradesh spreads over an area of nearly 23,700 sq km and accounts for 42.5 per cent of the state's total area on its north-eastern fringe. Administratively, the district of Kinnaur and Lahaul-Spiti, and the Bharmaur and Pangi tehsils of Chamba district comprise the belt. Tribals of the Himachal Pradesh form a contiguous belt to the extreme north east of the State. These are the far hinterlands behind mountain passes and are most inaccessible area in the state with an average altitude of 10,000 ft above the mean sea level. Chopra (1964) described the tribal lands of Himachal 'the last inhabited valley on Indian side of the frontier with Tibet lies enmeshed in the great tangle of mountains, the greatest in the world, which is known as the Western Himalayas'. Tribal areas like Kinnaur, Spiti and Lahaul, the first in particular, adjoin sensitive international borders and development of men and material should not lose sight of this fact. There is poor awareness of many things locally, and development of farsighted, wise and capable leadership among the tribals themselves is urgently called for (Negi 1976: 5).

Himachal tribes those constitute 5.6 per cent of the total population of the state according to the Census 2011. In comparison to the tribes of the other states, Himachal tribes are developed having better accessibility to the infrastructure as compared to the other tribes of the V Schedule. Communication and transport connectivity is available till the last point of the tribal area belt. In addition to the school facilities, there are government degree colleges in these areas. Primary health centres and community health centres are provided by the government to give them health services at the door steps. Besides these positivities, Himachal tribes in general, and Kinnaur particular, have an identity that is based on the overlapping of traditional and modern variables. Their endogamous nature is traditional variable, literacy among the tribes, i.e. 77.10 per cent is modern variable these are examples of the continuum and change in tribal society of Himachal. It is also evident from the social, economic and political institutions and their functioning in the tribal area. Social and economic system indicates the progressive and democratic attitude of the society where gender equality prevails. On the contrary to their progressive outlook social rigidity dominance of caste, class and gender-in-equality in political sphere questions the democratic ethos of the tribal society of the state. Himachal tribal is near to Hinduisation mainly. Christianity is less popular in the area.

Tribes, in most of the cases in Himachal Pradesh too, the aboriginal settlers, have been in place since time immemorial. The nomadic buffalo-raising Gujjars seem to have been an extraneous addition of the latter half or so of this century (Negi, in Gupta 1998: 101).

Scheduled Tribes of Himachal Pradesh represent a marked difference in their way of life as distinguished from other communities inhabiting this region. Not only this, even the lifestyle of one Scheduled Tribe differs from the other Scheduled Tribes in other parts of the country. Scheduled Tribes of the Himachal Pradesh inhabit the inaccessible part of the region, the geo-physical isolation of these tribal communities in sequestered in mountain valleys of the Western Himalayas. They have been isolated altogether from the main stream of the socio-cultural development of the mainland since centuries. Geographical factor has thus, been one of the main reasons for the evolution of the localised socio-cultural customs and tradition of their own. Moreover, each Scheduled Tribe of this region can be identified with specific geographical region (Kinnaur, Lahaul Spiti, Bharmaur and Pangi) and as such the area of their activities normally restricted to their particular limit. Nonetheless, there are some Scheduled Tribe communities like Gaddis and Gujjars who, although possess nomadic character, are associated with Bharmaur and Kilar areas of the Chamba district. They are always seen roaming with their quadrupled wealth in the pasture lands around Shivalik and elsewhere. Some of the Kinnauras and Lahulas also established their secondary habitats in the Shimla hills and Kullu respectively in order to further their mercantile pursuits.

Historically each Scheduled Tribe in this region is a separate entity in itself. Such tribal communities settled in the particular geographical limit in the area at different times. Inhabitants of Kinnaur and Lahaul Spiti districts are the earliest settlers whereas Gaddi and Gujjar made inroads to their present habitat recently during medieval period from the main land. Gaddis and Gujjars had been influenced by the predominating religious beliefs of that time and as such the religious sacraments are reflected in their marriage and other ceremonies. Since the native people of Kinnaur and Lahaul Spiti remained away from the Brahmanic influence of the plains and as such secular character in their marriage and other social ceremonies reflects. Thus, the time gap in the settlement of different tribal communities in the region had influenced the socio-cultural life of these people to a greater extent.

Ethnologically also the Scheduled Tribes of the Himachal Pradesh are different from one and other, e.g. Kinnaur and Spiti tribals are more akin to the Mongolian group of human race whereas the Gaddis and Gujjars found their resemblance with the people of main land. Likewise, Kinnauras and Lahulas are considered to profess the trademanship qualities of the Mongolian race and as such lead settled life whereas, Gaddis and Gujjars are basically shepherds and they are migratory communities. Thus, the ethnic characters of the Scheduled Tribes of Himachal are clearly visible in their way of life (Kapur 1993: 17). Tribals living in three pockets are known as Lahaulas, Pangwals and Kinnauras. Ethnologically there are numerous sub groups among them. In Lahaul: Sangwal, Bodh, Jads in Bharmaur and Pangi Gaddis and Gujjars are common name. Khas (Khoshiya), Khampa, Kanet all these communities are common in the Kinnnaur. These communities are endogamous groups. Marriage alliances are also restricted to their own communities. Their social structures are also heterogeneous. Stratification patterns are different from each other. Communities having different origins could be the reason behind these variations. Bodhs and Khampas migrated from Tibet. Gujjars are mainly from Gujarat. Kanets are mixed breed of Rajputs and indigenous people. Present tribe life is the result of evolutionary changes. According to Nathan (1997: 3), 'There were periods of accretion of small changes (say, the Vedic period, or within tribal systems), and there were also subsequent periods when these small changes in the ways of living, relating to each other and even making sense of things'. To understand the tribal society it is imperative to understand its historiography.

Historiography of Himachal Tribes

The geological explorations point to the fact that about two million years ago, there existed some form of human life in the foothills of Himachal. In the earliest stages, man must have been actively engaged in hunting and fruit gathering. He was mainly banking on the natural resources for his living and for his habitat, he explored the areas near the rivers having natural vegetation to cater his needs. The early man had accessibility to the stone as tool for hunting animals. Its evidence was found in the Markanda, Sirsa-Satluj valleys. These developments seem to be at least forty thousand years old. The pre-history of Himachal Pradesh is the history of migration of people from the Indian plains and from central Asia. In the very early times, outside the Indus Valley the Indo-Gangetic plain was inhabited by Proto-Austroloid known as Mundas speaking Kolarian people. These people were pushed forward as per compulsion and necessity. They seem to have fled northward into the present Himachal region. These people were divided into the groups such as Kols, Khasas, Dagis and Panis. Historically Kol people were the first one to inhabit the Himachal region. Possibly Halis and Chanals of the Western Himalayas and the Damangs and Chamangs of Kinnaur and Lahaul-Spiti are the remnants of this race. All the descendants of these earlier comers are the low castes of the present Himachal society.

Indo Aryans and Indo Mongoloids

After the Mundas, second group of the people of the Indo-Aryan origin arrived in this Himalayan region is about 2000 BC. They were known as Khasas and they claimed to be Aryans who left their original home in search of the new shelter for themselves and pastures for their animals.

They reached these areas and to make their home. Khasa is considered to be Kshatriyas, more ostensibly a warrior class. Gradually they started following the eating habits and life style which was more in consonance with the local conditions. They maintained their supremacy on the Kols of the area. In the hierarchical order of the society, they assumed the superior position than who were already living there. Khasas lived an organised life based on the formal power structures. Village was the unit of the community life. At the village level they had headman who was known as 'Mavans' or 'Mavi'. Its simple meaning was strong man. In the context of organised life, 'a person who possess capability to manage the community'. Every Mavana had jurisdiction over a certain land and he was responsible for its governance. It was a competitive system. The stronger Mavana whenever got the opportunity tried to defeat the weaker one. Later on these small units developed into the tribal republics. Practice of fraternal polyandry was practiced by Khasa in the regions Kinnaur, Chamba and some areas of Lahaul-Spiti. D.N. Majmudar (1962) also supports the view that the fraternal polyandry was in practice in these areas. This practice in the present tribal areas is followed but gradually with the changing conditions it is losing its past glory. Khasa is known in the tribal areas by different nomenclatures. In all the tribal areas they enjoy the status of the higher caste in Himachal tribal region. Another race Mangolian people settled in Himachal are mentioned as Kiratas and Bhots in literature. They belong to Mangolian race. They follow Buddhism. Their economy is based on the livestock rearing, shifting cultivation and trade practice.

With the rise of dynastic rule in the North India, evolutionary system of migration from other places over powered by the interventions of the Mauryan dynasty in this area. Chandragupta Maurya's (340–298 BCE) was the first ruler of the Mauryan Empire. Before the advent of Chandragupta, India was composed of number of small independent states, with the exception of Magadha kingdom, a realm that controlled most of the Northern India. His ambition was to expand his boundaries to the natural boundaries of Bharat and unify India for the first time in Indian history. After the departure of Alexander, they took full advantage of the prevailing situation and made alliances with the Himalayan head, Paravtaka and made fresh recruitments from the local people. Literary sources well established that hilly region of Himachal Pradesh formed a part of the Mauryan kingdom. Ashoka's penetration is evident from the inscriptions of Rummandi Nigilihwa. After the disintegration of the Mauryan Empire, the arrival of Indo-Greeks in the Himachal is a debatable issue. Coins found in Arki Chamba, Una is an evidence of their arrival in the Himachal.

Emergence of Tribal States in Himachal Region

After the decline of the great empires, local political identities became strong and many tribal states came into existence. These states had their indigenous political administrative set ups. Term 'tribe' is used in the sense these small territories had their distinct identity and they remained rooted to their unique social and economic practices. They were not barbarians as the term in common is defined by some world class dictionaries. They had primitive economy. Mahabharta, Ramayana and Panani's Ashtadhyayi has reference of the *Janapadas* in Himachal. Katyayana states that there were two types of *Janapadas*: (i) monarchical or *ekaraja*, and (ii) republican or *sangh*. Adumbara was a tribe in the present Kangra strategically it was important area and trade centre. Its coinage confirms its prosperity. Coins found in the area are silver coins. This tribe fell before the Kushana Empire emerged. Vemaki was another tribe which had its territory near the Trigarta. Vrishni tribe was a republican tribe. It was a democratic republic. It is mentioned in Panini's Ashtadhyayi. This tribe might have settled along with Kultas and Adumbaras in the foot-hills of Himalayan region. Puru was one of the tribes which find mention in the Rigveda. Puruava people were inhabitants of hill region of Himachal Pradesh near Kultas. Trigara was the oldest tribal state of the Himachal region. The earliest reference to this tribal state is found in Panini's Ashtadhyayi. It's numismatic evidence is available from a solitary coin of first century AD as a republic. Kulta tribe finds its mention in the Bhishma Parva of Mahabharat. It was the second oldest tribe of Himachal region. Kultas ruled over the upper valley of Beas, the present Kullu Valley. The Kultas lost its republican character in all probabilities during the beginning of the Christian era. Kuninda republic included present Kinnaur Shimla and Sirmour. It is referred in the *Vishnu Purana, Vayu Purana* and *Markandeya Purana.* Rise of tribal states in the region might be the result of weaker central power. These tribal republics' prosperity indicates that they were sovereign communities and had flourished economy. They cannot be categorised tribes in the present sense when the tribals are considered backward economically and socially. These early communities fall in the tribe category because of their distinct cultural and political identity.

Gupta Empire and Himachal Region

These tribes flourished till the Gupta empire was consolidated. Gupta emperors, particularly Samudragupta known as the Napoleon of India, intended to annex the far away territories stretching up to the natural boundaries of Bharat. Himachal had number of tribal states over ruled by the Guptas during the Gupta period. These republics known as *Janapadas* had their own governing institutions. With the influence of the over lords they eventually started following the practices of the Guptas, consolidated their power structures and organised as monarchies. According to literary evidence Audumbaras and Kunidas, totally disintegrated completely and new dynasties came into existence at Chamba, Kullu, Sirmaur and Bushahar region. In the middle of fifth century AD Central Asian tribe namely Huns, later known as Gujjars, settled in Punjab. Their king according to Rajatrangini was defeated united princes in Kashmir. Some of the Hunas might have escaped to the hills and were absorbed to the Hindu society. Those who were not absorbed followed the nomadic life. Present Gujjar community is their descendants. These upheavals in the area led to the rise of local principalities in the area. Harsha was one of the strongest ruler of north India after Guptas who ruled from 606 to 648 AD after Guptas. He established great empire over northern Himalayas to the Nerbudda river (Bahadur 1978; Chauhan 1998). He had control over the Himachal region, as per the references in Rajatrangini and travelogue of Heun Tsang Chinese pilgrim. Harsha controlled these kingdoms through his officials of the rank of today's governor. He was representative of the Harsha in the far flung kingdoms. Jalandhar, Bharmaur, Kulta, Spiti and Shrughna were the main kingdoms. With the early medieval periods feudatories and emergence of the Rajput states in Rajasthan pushed those feudal lords to the North. These sections supplement the new migrations to the Himachal region and new political paradigms began to emerge, with the coming of the Rajputs in the area. New principalities came into existence before the Muslim invasions took place. Chiefs of these principalities were known as the Thakurs and Ranas. They were brave people (warriors) known as Rajputs. These chiefs were at war with each other to prove their superiority and to seize the land of other chief. Sometimes they invited their other Rajput chiefs from the plains to assist them in the war. In this region Kangra, Jaswan, Guler, Siba, Datarpur, Nurpur, Chamba, Suket, Mandi, Kullu, Bilaspur (Kahlur), Hindur (Nalagarh) were the main Rajput states. Rajput states did not change much. Basic reason for the linear development of these states was the geographical conditions and tough terrain of the area and natural boundaries. Other reason was their racial and cultural homogeneity. Most of them were the migrants from the plain areas and they had feeling of fraternity. They wanted to maintain their control over their predecessors in the area. Muslim rulers in the early medieval period and Mughal made endeavours to penetrate in the Kangra, but their invasions were superficial and no drastic change took place in the socio-economic and political system of the Kangra. In Chamba and Sirmaur, Mughals penetrated in the area but they were not successful to maintain constant control over these states. Muslim rule had less impact on the Himachal society.

With the coming of the Britishers and their realisation that area was of strategic importance they focused on the Himachal region. Strategically, the area was of great importance as it was a wedge between the Gurukha possessions and territories of Maharaja Ranjit Singh. It was potential value of revenue. Climatically, it was suitable for them as its climate was similar to their own country. It had commercial importance also for promoting commercial interests in Tibet and China. When the East India Company occupied the Shimla Hill States in 1815–16, the principalities were small feudal states. They were at war with each other. Medieval practices and dominance of land lords were prevalent in socio-political system. Caste, class and patriarchal institutions were the determining factors of the roles. With the coming of the Britishers and opening avenues in the economic, social and political fields the society underwent gradual transformation, pace of transformation was slow. It was evident at the time of the national movement. T(t)he nationalist forces: the Congressmen and the Praja Mandalists from Shimla and outside the states started propaganda against the Chiefs and the government. This led to the politicisation of the subjects of the states; as a result even classes belonging to the lower strata of the society became bold and demanded end not only to autocracy, but also their share in the administration (Datta 1984).

History of Himachal region indicates that Himachal since the ancient times is the land of the migrants. People came here from different places and augmented the social culture fabric of the society. Some of the institutions persisted throughout the history of the Himachal region. Village always remains the unit of the governance and the states were small. This area had never been a consolidated power centre in the region it might be due to the geographical conditions. During the dynasty rule at different points of time Himachal had its overlords they exerted control over the local principalities, kingdoms through their own representatives. This kind of the relationship had little impact on the internal working of the society. The states which were called Janapadas or tribal states by some of the scholars, were the states which had their distinct socio-political identity. These societies could not have been tribal in the present context when the tribal are considered economically and socially backward. Medieval practices gave concrete shape to some of the institutions. These institutions provided base for the practices in the socio-economic and political fields. These practices dominated the system persistently. Some of the practices are not compatible to the democratic principles of equality, liberty fraternity and social justice. It has become difficult to challenge those medival practices or reconstruct them according to the emerging needs.

Conclusion

Tribes constitute a small but important segment of the Himachal society. These are descendants of the earliest inhabitants of the subcontinent. They contributed to the variety and riches of cultural forms in the country. Over the centuries, they have preserved a distinctive style of life in terms of quality life and cultural ethos.

7

Kinnaura Tribe of Himachal

Kinnauras

Kinner Desh has been mentioned in the Vedas, Puranas, and in the succeeding literature. Tradition of the Kinner desh refers to a time when this part of the land was far larger than the district of today. Kinnauras means the inhabitants of Kinnaur. It is also pronounced as Kinnawar, Kanaur, Koomkawar and Kinnauras.

Mythological Base of Origin of Kinnauras

The word 'myth' comes from ancient Greek word 'mythos', meaning 'speech, narrative fiction, myth, plot'. In Anglicised form, this Greek word began to be used in English (and was like wise adapted into other European languages) in the early nineteenth century, in a much narrower sense, as scholarly term for 'traditional story typically involving to super-natural beings or forces, which embodies and provides an explanation, aetiology, or justification for something such as the early history of society, a religious belief or ritual, or a natural phenomenon'. Myth in general can be defined as 'a traditional story, especially one concerning the early history of a people or explaining a natural or social phenomenon, and typically involving super natural beings or events'. There are many tribes and castes in India which claim their origin from divine sources and the Kinners (Kinnauras, Kimpurusha, Khas or Khasia) is one such tribe. Famous Sanskrit classic 'Amarkosha/Amarkosa' mentions the Gandharvas, Yakshas, Vidyadharas, Apsaras, Sidhas, Guhayakas, Pishachas, Bhutas and Kinners.

According to 'Bhagvat Purana', Kinnaur trace their origin to the shadow of Lord Brahma. Yet another legend says that they have sprung from the toe of Brahama along with the Yakshasa. But according to Bhavrico Upanishad, Devi created them with Brahma, Vishnu, Maruta, Rudra, Gandharva and Asura. In Mahabharata, they have been grouped with the Gandharvas while in 'Matasaya-Purana' their kinship with Kiratas and the Yakshasa has been focused upon (Saklani 1998: 74).

Encyclopedia of the Religion and Ethics depicts the Kinners with 'horse head' and the Kimpurashas with 'horse body'. Probably such descriptions led to the epithet of Kimpurashas, that has Sanskrit origin meaning '*Kim*' (what kind of) and '*Nara* or *Purusha*' (human beings). The word (Kinner = *Kim* + *Nara*) also means 'what kind of strange persons they are'. In the mythological and legendary accounts, Kinners are described as a distinct race of demigods, somewhere between human beings as Gods. They are described in various forms. Some mention them half man and half birds. Some other references depict them with a human body and a horse's head. Kinners find mentions not only in Hindu religious books, but also in Jains and Buddhist scriptures. The Jain's religious books offer a classification of 'Neun Dev Yoni's' in which one category is that of Kinners. Similarly the classification given by Buddhist scriptures includes as one of the races. The Brahminical classification included many categories. All these categories are now called Kinnauras, also known as 'Khas' or 'Khasia' (Balokhra 2011: 96).

The present official name of the district is Kinnaur. There are evidences which support the theory that whether it was king Kubera or Raja Indra or tradition of the Kinner Desh refers to the time when this part of the land was far larger than the district of today. Evidences from the Vedic and the other auxiliary sources show that the Gandharvas and Kinnauras were conceived to be composite creatures in pre-historic India of the Vedic period. According to the Puranas, 'at the foot of the mountain there is Somasila where the moon shines once a year. It also mentions a big city in Kailash Parvata among the residents of which the Kinnauras also figure' (Attri 2010: 167).

A large track of tribal areas of Himachal Pradesh belongs to Kinnaur or locally known as Kinnauras. Particularly, the area comprising of Kinnaur district and Kanawar Kothi of Kullu district is their traditional home. In the classical literature, they have been shown along with Gandharvas, Yaksas, Rakshasas, Vidyadharas, Uragas, etc. Except for Rakshasas, all the remaining races have been shown in good sense. These names, originally, implied classes of mythical belong, but later they indicated certain tribal people (Thakur 1997: 25).

The Kinnaura polity began in all probability under personal rule. At the time of formation of Himachal Pradesh on 15 April 1948, Kinnaur was already a part of the territory that comprised the state. Kinnaur continued to be part of Mahasu district till 1 May 1960 when Kinnaur was carved out as a separate district.

On 1 November 1966, Punjab state of that time was recognised with the formation of Haryana as a separate state. Lahaul Spiti, Kangra, Shimla and hill areas of Hoshiarpur district and Dalhousie of Gurdaspur district were merged into Himachal Pradesh constituting the four districts, namely Kullu, Lahaul-Spiti, Kangra and Shimla in Himachal Pradesh. Dalhousie was merged into Chamba district and Nalagarh in Mahasu district as one of the tehsils.

Kinnaur as the sixth district came into being on 1 May 1960. Kinnaur district was formed by carving the entire Chini tehsil and 14 villages from Rampur tehsil of Mahasu district. There was no change in the jurisdiction of the state as a result of the passing of the States Reorganization Act, 1956. For administrative purpose, however, certain changes within the districts of Chamba, Bilaspur, Sirmour and Mahasu with regard to jurisdiction were carried out (Attri 2010: 168).

Kinnauras (or Kinnor) live in the valley around Kinnar Kailash in the frontier district of Kinnaur (Himachal Pradesh). They are said to be the descendent of the ancient tribe of Kinnaur which is referred to in Indian mythology as celestial beings and shown in Indian iconography as images around a deity like Siva, Vishnu or other gods and goddesses.

Kinnaura tribe finds mention in every religious book and sculptures of Hindus. As per Rahul Sankritayana's version, the Kinner or Kimpurusha (what kind of strange persons were they) was the bad name given to the enslaved and defeated Dasa. They have been immortalised by frescoes of Ajanta painted by Japanese, Chinese, Mongolians and Tibetans while the Mahabharta has their mention and Kalidas has written about them. However their descendants, the Kinner population, are limited to the present Kinnaur district only (quoted in Chauhan 1998; 109–10). Kinnaura is the single largest Scheduled Tribe which inhabits the district of Kinnaur (Monga 1998: 372). They play music and perform dance in the *darbar* of a deity. Kinnauras belong to the Mongoloid race but there has been intermingling with the Aryan, Dravidian and central Asian racial groups. Therefore, like the Pangwals and Lahulas, the Kinnauras are also not pure Mangolians. It is also curious that the Kinnauras living below the Kanam are mostly Hindus and have Aryan features. Above Kanam, Kinnauras are Buddhist and in features they resemble to the Tibetans. The Kinnauras of Sangla Valley have more alpine feature, faces are flat, cheekbones are high, and nose and lips slightly thick. Skin is ruddy and fair. In other places, in the main valley of the Sutlej from Tranda to Kanam, the Kinnauras have mixed Aryan and Mongoloid characteristics.

Kinnauras undertake diverse economic activities, they are pastoral people and rear sheep and goats, besides being involved in agricultural activities. In present times, they are also engaged in horticulture, agriculture and hydro power projects. Like the Gaddis of Chamba, in winter, they move down to the Bilaspur, Solan and Sirmour. They have hereditary rights for grazing their herds in that area. In summers, they go to the high land pastures in Kinnaur and Spiti. A few move to Garhwal area as well. In March–April they start their homeward trek along with their herds. Earlier, the elders along with some of the young people used to stay at home to support their family in winter in Kinnaur. Nowadays a large number remains at home for the winter. In fact, the Kinnauras have switched over to various other professions; quite a few are active orchardists now. Some are engaged in the collection of honey, condiments and other herbs. Others are involved in trade, transportation, labour work and government jobs. The kinnauras are primarily agriculturists and their subsidiary occupations are weaving, spinning, silversmith, wood carving (carpentry) and artistic metalware manufacturing. They grow wheat, barley, millet, maize, rice, vegetables and pulses. Their class character also serves as base for the stratification of the society. People possessing land and orchards form the elite section of the society due to their financial position. They have an upper hand in the formal social and political power structures as well as in traditional informal power structures. Service providers among the Kinnauras whose livelihood depends on the labour, belong to the lower sections of the society. With the passage of time these stratification patterns have become rigid. Social mobility is not possible due to caste character of the society. Caste pattern is not similar to the Hindu caste system. Hindu caste system (based on four castes) is not practiced in the Kinnaur community. Mainly there are two castes and both have their specified roles. Being conservative in social practices they follow untouchability, endogamy in matrimonial relations within sub-sections of their society. Kinnaura society is a caste ridden society.

Their houses are simple and made of wood, stone and mud. Their architect styles and use of local materials protect them from the adverse weather conditions. Nowadays people started using cement and bricks to build huge RCC structures which are not suited to the local geography. They are fond of gadgets, and electric heaters, gas heater and other electric appliances, gradually these gadgets are replacing tandoor which was important part of the family accessories. Tandoor was introduced by the missionaries in the nineteenth century when they came from Europe to spread Christianity in the far flung areas. They also made some efforts to educate the local people and to sensitise them about health and hygiene issues. In the traditional houses, the granaries are located nearby and are square wooden structure built on a base of rock or stone to protect the grain from the dampness. A house is aligned with *Bhoj Patra* (birch) to save it from insects. Some houses are sloped and roofed with local irregular slates or wooden planks. The village chiefs earlier were the Negis. Negi was title given to the person who excelled in the one or other field or having cordial relations with the higher authorities, moneyed person or a person who enjoyed social acceptability because of his behaviour with the people. Thakurai in simple terms was a system in which a person enjoyed the authority and was also responsible for the administration of the area. Area under Thakurai was a group of villages.

Traditional Power Structure of Kinnaura Tribe

In this area, there were 21 Thakurais (person holding power at the Prangna level). The Thakurais were in constant conflict with each other. Ultimately all the Thakurais were defeated by the Kamaru Thakurai. Thakur of Kamaru emerged as the strongest, and annexed the territories of all Thakurais, some time after the fall of Kannauj empire. Its reign continued till the Bhushar state came into existence. Thakurai as a political system was dominated by the upper caste. At the village level, during the days of Thakurais, 'Charas' system was in vague. This institution managed the local affairs based on the two way communication from bottom to top and top to bottom. Local people had faith in Charas. They treated Charas as their headman. With the decline of Thakurais, the institution of Devta emerged as the power centre. Charas who was unanswerable to the Thakurais now came to be known as 'Shu-Charas'. The prefix Shu stands for *Devta*. Shu-Charas was the representative of the local Devta, working on the directions of the Shu (Devta). He administered the village according to the directions of the Devta of the area. Informal power institutions still play a significant role in the tribal area. People have faith in the Devta. They do not dare to defy his instructions in their day to day life. During the field study, local people accepted the authority of Devta as an important institution and their unflinching faith in his powers. With the introduction of the democratic set up in the tribal societies, two parallel system are working simultaneously. People elect constitutional bodies under the PESA Act. They also have informal local power centres. Sometimes these two power systems overlap and people give importance to the traditional institutions. Disputes are decided by the traditional institutions (Devta, Khoomini). Khoomini is a traditional institution where elderly people are involved in settling the disputes among the villagers. Issues are taken to the courts or formal judicial institutions very rarely.

Social Life of Kinnauras

Kinnauras have simple food habits. They take nutritious food and their food items include local cereals, vegetables, herbs and honey. Kinnauras eat bread made from wheat, barley, maize and millet flour. Otherwise the flour is converted into a pudding and eaten with soups, dal, meat or vegetables. Butter tea is popular drink among them and is consumed frequently. A kind of apricot soup is prepared which is greatly relished. Kinnauras prepare rice beer and liquor from barley, maize, millet, chuli (apricot) and grapes. Anguri and the Nesang brandy are the famous spirits of Kinnaur. Anguri is prepared from the locally grown grapes. The Nesang brandy is made from barley and has a distinct aroma and taste. It comes from a place called Nesang. It is gaining popularity among the non-Kinnauras. Due to the rich nutrition and medicinal value, the wild fauna and flora of the area and their cereals are much sought after internationally. Government is taking steps to educate the tribes regarding their precious heritage.

Schools have been opened at short distances in the area to provide education at the door step to the people in the area. Just like population in the mainstream, the tribals also lay special emphasis on education. Those who can afford, send their children to the cities. Their wards stay in Shimla for schooling or they are sent to the boarding schools. Kinnaura tribals excel in education. Those who cannot effort to send their wards outside for education send them to the local schools. Some of the bureaucrats had their schooling in the local schools. This tribe is a progressive tribe that adapts to change without ignoring their own cultural and social practices. Their family system has certain consistent practices. They live in joint families due to their professional limitations but now they have started living in other parts of the states as nuclear families. In fact they prefer living as a joint family so that they can maintain undivided property. Family members who live in the urban areas gladly provide support to the children of other family members who stay back in the villages and take care of the property. They do not harbour family rivalries. They have strong fraternity feeling. To keep their property collective they used to practice polyandry. With the passage of time this practice is losing its relevance. Otherwise its a polyandrous tribe. A fraternal type of polyandry is still in existence though the present generation does not prefer it. Dependence on land resources has been on a decline. The younger generation is joining service sector, private sector and has tried hand at business also. The economic system has been altered as consequence of these recent developments. It is one of the major causes of change in the marriage system.

Among Kinnauras too, developmental benefits have not been distributed equally. Due to class and caste division it is only miniscule minority which has been benefited by the education and other development schemes provided to the Kinnaura tribe (Panchani 1994: 86). Those who are not economically well off are not able to harness the benefits of the reservation. Only the moneyed class send their children to the good institutions and get selected for the services.

Kinnauras are the most beautiful people and a number of anecdotes can be traced from the Holy Scriptures; the most chivalrous race of Devas was lured by the damsels of this land. Kinners were the most wonderful singers. They, therefore, found their place at Durbar of lord Indra, the king of Devas. They are expert in music and dance. Dances are famous for their slow rhythmical steps and for their musical effects. No festival or ritual is complete without the performance of a dance. Dancers move to the rhythms of their musical instruments like drums, nagaras, shehnai, bugjal, flute, ransingha, karnal, etc. Despite these traditional instruments, these days modern music system has been becoming popular in the marriage parties and other festivals. The musical instruments are played by a particular clan, popularly known as Bajantry. They are the best instrumentalists but are considered to be of the lower status in society. Among all the dances of Kinnaur, Kayang is the most fascinating. It is performed in several ways. Different dances are performed on different occasions. Of course, there are a few dances which can be enjoyed on all occasions and in all seasons. Community dances are very common among the Kinnauras. Male and female equally and enthusiastically participate in these dances. There is no gender discrimination. Women in the area also consume local wines. Social equality and free culture of the Kinnaura community is an indicator of the tribal culture. Among the tribals, women generally are more open and enjoy equality as compare to the main stream society of India. 'Communities have been more gender equal and more communitarian than our (mainstream) own', this statement regarding the tribal society by Nathan is true about the Kinnaura tribe (Nathan 1994).

People are modest, unpretentious and decent as far as their dealing and behaviour is concerned. They are honest and industrious. Thieves and robbers are unheard in the area and an individual's words may be implicitly relied upon in distrust and suspicion. Females are more attuned to the labour in the fields and cultivation while the males either assist them or go away in search for better avenues. They are open to strangers and there is no 'parda' system prevalent in the society. Their hospitability is exemplary. Often their openness and frankness is misunderstood by the strangers and a number of such references can be traced from the books written by foreigners (Jerath 1995: 27).

Customs

Birth Customs

In the past as soon as the prospective mother gets labour pains, she is confined to *'Khudd'* (Cowshed). *'Dai'* (indigenous midwife) looks after the mother as well as the new born. Cutting of the umbilical cord and disposal of placenta is her responsibility. However, this practice is fast diminishing, with the ever increasing medical awareness among the Kinnaur tribe. People prefer to go to the hospitals for delivery. There is no tradition of singing songs on the birth of a child. In the area people do not have gender bias at the time of birth of a child. Female child is treated equal to the male child. There are some ritual and festivals which are performed by the parents after the birth of the male child in the family. Community feast figure chiefly in the least. In Ropa village all families blessed with sons offer one goat collectively to the village deity on Ukhyang festival.

Death Customs

Like all parts of the world, there are traditional death customs related to the disposal of the dead body. Mainly there are three practices: '*dubant*' (drowning), '*phukant*' (burning) and '*bhakhant*' (eating by vultures, birds, etc.). However, now cremation through burning is practiced in Kinnaura society. Dead body is placed on '*dursa*' (pyre made of wood) at the cremation ground and the same is lit by a close relative of the deceased. Then on the same evening, the act of '*thuning*' is performed in which the bereaved members throw a mixed pudding prepared from loaves and pulses on the roof of their houses with the belief that through crows and other birds the food would reach to the departed soul. Family remains in mourning for one year. The inmates of the house take simple vegetarian food for next thirteen days and thereafter on any convenient night the bereaved family throws a feast (with liquor and good food) to the villagers. After drinking and eating the food villagers sing and dance. It is considered the end of the mourning in the clan.

Marriage Customs

Marriage among the Kinnauras is a community event symbolic of the union of the two families. In the law relating to social reforms, Bushahr, 1989 (Sambat) marriage in Kinnaur is defined as the relationship between a man and woman which is recognised by the law of the land in force or custom of the land. However, no Vedic rites such as going round the fire, etc. are followed in the solemnisation of marriages in the Kinnaur. Following are the forms of marriages in Kinnaur:

1. Janetang or Janeekang: It is the only legal form of arranged marriage (wedding).
2. Damtangshish, Bennang-hachis or Jushis: It is love marriage.
3. Darosh, Dub-dub, Dab-Dab, Nymasha-depang, Nymsha-lemo, Ashish, Huchis or Khuchis: It is marriage by forceful or consented capture.
4. Haar: It is enticing away someone's wife (Monga 1998: 376).

Fraternal Polyandry

In Kinnaur fraternal polyandry is in vogue and is a delicate subject. It was prolonged because of the historical reasons and economic compulsions of the society. In this type of marriage the elder brother in a family marries a woman, who becomes the common wife of all the brothers in the family. Older people of the area defend this practice on the ground that it has kept the family a closely knit entity. It has prevented over-population and the sub-division or fragmentation of the small agricultural holdings. In former times several brothers in a family were never at home together at any particular time, but now they can all be there, as they get work near their homes, this has become a constant source of quarrel among them making the life of the lady of the house miserable. Interaction with the mainstream society and less dependence on the land resources are also additional causes of polyandry system becoming less popular among the Kinnauras. In fraternal polyandry common marriage of brothers of the family was solemnised with a single girl irrespective of the age of grooms. Generally eldest brother had the say in this type of the marriage. A proposal of the marriage was put up by the groom's family through middleman of repute. If accepted by the parents of the bride the parents or the middle man would approach the family of the bride with token of gift like an ornament, golden nose ring or a necklace which would be accepted by the parents of the bride on her behalf. Generally a bottle of home brewed liquor was also carried along with the massage which was readily accepted and distributed among all the members present followed by the worship of the village Gods and Goddess. A Lama is called who recites certain hymns toward off the ill spirits. Even before the settlement of the marriage Lamas are consulted so as to get the prediction of the good, lasting marriage. On a decided date the eldest brother along with a few kith and kins would leave for the bride's home. They are received by the family members of the bride and given a feast. The whole night they sing and dance and the next day the groom with bride and bride party would leave for their home where the party was received at the door by the elderly ladies, mother and other relatives of the bridegroom. Merry-making continues for the next three days when people of the locality are invited over a feast. All the brothers who would be the husbands of the bride used to be adorned with bridal turban, connecting it with string attire of the bride and certain pledges are conducted in favour of the bride so that she would be recognised as the lady of the family. Because of the several drawbacks, the trend of polyandry and polygamy are gradually diminishing. Traditional marriage system has many positive points, for example, the land in possession of family always remain intact. Chances of problems of the distribution and division of the land property are rare. Fraternal polyandry system was also one of the compulsions. Due to sparse resources every male member was not able to have independent family. Hence they preferred this traditional practice. The whole family used to work as a unit and the lady at the helm of the affairs was never deserted by anybody in the society. She did not use to see the bad days of widow-ship as long as any one of the brother is alive (Parmar 1975: 75).

Monogamy is the order of the day. People are educated and they believe polyandry has lost its relevance. Land is not the only source of family income. It is supplemented by the service sector and business activities in the area. Marriage is arranged by the parents and the process is almost the same. Now people are adopting the nuclear family system. Monogamy is popular among the new generation. Those living in the remote areas still have retained their traditional values, but on the whole the area located nearby the main roads are turning their grab speedily (Jerath 1995: 30). Divorce among the Kinnauras has been recognised as an accepted practice since ancient times. It is evident from the fact that the 'Haar' marriage is recognised in the society. A wife in Haar marriage gets the legal status of wife which is possible only if her first marriage is dissolved. In other words, when the second husband compensate the husband of the first marriage, first marriage stands dissolved without which the wife could not attain the status of wife in the second marriage. This shows the existence of the concept of divorce among the Kinnaura society. Except in the case of 'Haar' main reason for divorce is domestic quarrels. In the wake of dispute, only between the husband and wife, the middleman, generally those who arrange the marriage are again requested to intervene (Chandra 1992: 158). Hindu Marriage Act 1955 (No. of 1955) providing for the divorce, being inapplicable to the members of Scheduled Tribes, only traditional type of divorce is applicable which is called Shingtakshmig or Razinama in which both husband and wife break the piece of dried wood and marriage expenses are paid to the husband by wife's parents. The utensils, ornaments and udanang (money collected at the time of marriage on the behalf of wife's relatives side) given at the time of marriage are returned by the husband (Kapur 1993: 71).

However, during the field study, Janetang, Bennang or Damchalchish, Darosh, noticed common among the younger generations of the Kinnaura tribal society against the age old custom of the polyandry. This change is a welcome step in the improved socio-economic conditions of the people in the light of the development activities undertaken by the government and free mixing of tribal with the non-tribal population due to the improved means of communication and spread of educational activities.

Food and Drink

In Kinnaur main food is called *'Khaoo'*. It consists of two main diets, lunch and dinner. *'Shill'* is the supper and these days people have started taking breakfast in the morning, even elderly people also use the word 'breakfast'. Barley, ogala, phaphra, chini, chalai, wheat, rice, maize, kada and bami are the commonly used cereals of the Kinnaur district. Out of these cereals *Roti, Poltu, Aalu rang Chutney, Brasskan, Choyakan rang Brasu hod, Dup, Kodro roti rang ragkan, Yud, Phanitang, Zorbokan rang Ral, Mar rang Dhu, Remo thukpa, Sutrale, Kanoi, Ral, Skur and Sunpole* (Joote in Pooh subdivision) are some important dishes prepared with special care and ingredients. *Joote* (*or Sunpole*) is prepared like Jalebis of the ogala flour in frying pan. They are consumed as refreshment with tea during festive occasions *Kaoni*, similar to saltish barfi, a sweet is considered as sacred food taken on religious festivals and is also distributed to Harijans on such occasions. *Ral* (or Rice) is taken either as boiled rice or *Ralu-thupa* (Khichari), the latter being a mixture of rice, water, salt, spices and animal fat. Sutrale is a festive dish.

Drinking is quite common among men in Kinnaur. Women, barring as an offering of the deity as a religious practice, do not drink but drinking among the women folk is not considered taboo like the society in general. However, distillation is the business of the women folk. Practically every household is a mini distillery, for which a permit is granted for personal use by the appropriate authorities. Alcohol has an important place in the life of the Kinnauras and is an essential article required for the performance of any Puja and in the worship of deities. Distilled or fermented liquor is prepared for the house-hold by employing indigenous method and by using all kinds of the fruits and grains. Arak (rakh or Phasur) and Dakhangu-phasur (Anguri) are prepared by distillation, the latter especially at Ribba. Ningo, Chhang (Shudung) and Doja are prepared by fermentation. Chhang prepared from barley is extensively used in Hangrung valley. Ghanti is the local wine of the Kinnaur prepared from barley, apple, apricot, nashpati and other cereals. Brandy is distilled in Nesang village (Sanan 1998: 62–63).

Dress and Ornaments

Dresses. Kinnauras are famous for their own distinctive dresses and ornaments. Traditional dress of the Kinnaura women resembles pannier worn by the English woman long back. Dresses used in Hangrang valley are clearly distinct from the dresses worn elsewhere in Kinnaur. Because of the cold climate in all parts of Kinnaur, people wear woollen clothes throughout the year. Originally three types of wool are available locally. *Byangiwool* has the longest staple of about five inches. *Lamboowool* is the soft wool from the first shearing of the lamb. *Desarwool* is of coarser quality and is from the sheep, which do not migrate. Both men and women wear *Thepang* (called *Kinnaurior Bushahri* or Himachali cap), which is decorated with the seasonal flowers and Chamkha. Kinnauri bride wear special cap in the marriage called *Kherthepang* or *Pradthepang* along with *chamkha* (oroxylum seeds). The men wear woollen shirts *Chamukurti*, long woollen coat/cloak *Chhuba* or *Chhoba* and woollen pyjama *Chamusutan* mostly of grey colour, sometimes white, but never black. Ladies wear woollen sari with a girdle *Dhori*, full sleeved blouse *Choli*, woollen rope *Gachang* and shawl *Chauli*. *Dhori* is a blanket that folds partly round the body and partly comes up around the shoulders and across the breasts, where it is fastened by a large metal broach (Ahluwalia 1998: 83).

Dark red or dark brown coloured clothes are preferred in Hangrang valley. The important garments of male dress are: (i) *Ragu* (shirt); (ii) *Ghoya* (woollen cloak); (iii) *Suluka* (waist coat); (iv) *Sutan* (woollen trousers); (v) *Shew* (cap); and (vi) *Kera* (woollen rope tied around waist). The important garments of female dress are: (i) *Ra-Ghaja* (ordinary shirt); (ii) *Golak* (also called Ghoye, Yangluk or Ligche) (woollen shawl); (iii) *Sutan* (woollen trousers); (iv) *Shew* (cap); and (v) *Kera* (woollen rope tied around waist). Children wear *Chutan*, which is akin to a baby shawl. Modernity has also affected the mode and kind of dresses of Kinnauras. Kinnaura dress is elegant and simple. Kinnauri people love to wear their dress. Occasionally they dress up according to their tradition in formal functions in the cities also. In marriages most of the people wear their own traditional dresses otherwise youngsters love to wear western costume and ladies wear regular suits.

Ornaments

Ornaments (thick bracelets, large ear-rings, heavy silver chains, various kinds of beads and precious stones) are the most valuable possession of Kinnauri women. They are generally made of silver and gold. Important head wearing ornaments made of silver are *Chak*, *Chiri*, *Tanol*, *Zuti*, *Pipla*, *Tunki* and *Dabmige*. Silver made *Mul*-u, *Kontai*, *Jumku*, *Tarimol*, *Kantae* and *Kontai* are ear wearing and gold made *Murkee*, *Tili*, *Launge*, *Balu*, *Kundoch* and *Balak* are nose wearing ornaments. The coral or precious stones made *Likcha* and *Shulikcha* and silver made Chandra-har are neck-wearing ornaments. The *Daglo* (Dakloo), *Kagun*, Gurshangling and *Digra* which are made of silver or gold are wrist wearing and silver made *Digra* (Deegra) and *Tomukch* are breast wearing ornaments. Kinnaura men do not use ornaments generally, but in the old days they used to wear *Daglo* (steel bangles) and *Botone-se-Shanglya* (silver chain with buttons). Men and shepherds of Upper Kinnaur usually possess *Chakman* (a piece of steel for striking fire), a knife, a hatchet, a smoking pipe (Hukka) and goats hair round waist. The women of the district previously used to go about laden with heavy jewellery like bracelets, large ear-ring, heavy silver chains, various kinds of beads and precious stones but there is a growing tendency among them to use comparatively lighter ornaments and thus silver ornaments are getting out of fashion. The modern young men and women, are however, discarding the use of traditional heavy jewellery (Mamgain 1971: 11).

Forest Wealth

Forest covered area in the district Kinnaur according to the forest department is 629 sq km, average 9.8 per cent of the total geographical area, viz. 6,401 sq km. The chief factor affecting the distribution and quality of forest vegetation are rain fall and elevation aspect. The forests of the Kinnaur have been classified into following 'types' according to 'Revised Survey of the Forest Types of India' (Champion and Seth 1968: 404).

Presently, *Pinus roxburghi, Pinus wallichiana, Cedrus deodara, Picea smithiana, Picea smithiana* and *Pinus gerardiana* form a broad belt of forest along both side of the Satluj valley and the side streams between the cliffs of the gorge below and alpine pastures and eternal snow above. On the left side of the valley northern exposures, forests come much lower down towards and river than they do on the right bank, while isolation of direct sunlight restricts the spread of vegetation. On the left side, the forests are particularly continuous. From the river-side at 3,500 feet to alpine pasture at 12,000 feet on the right base there are grass-lands and higher up are the forest belts. Along the side stream, however, the forests are well developed. Kinnaur was extremely rich in fauna but with the developmental activities like construction of buildings and road and increasing population, the density of fauna has diminished gradually. Blue sheep, Hill fox, Brown bear, Flying fox, European bat, Ghoral, Himalayan Langgur, Leopard, Panther, Musk deer and wolf, etc. some birds like Monal, Hawk, Eagle, Himalayan Crow, etc. are found in this region. Some reptiles like Indian Chameleon, Krait, Monitor Lizard, Common house Gecko, etc. are seen here and there. Trout is well known species of fish in Baspa River. However fishing is not a part of either food habit or amusement of the people.

It is unfortunate that the rich flora and fauna wealth of Kinnaur has been under threat from hydro electric power projects construction, widening of roads, illicit felling, soil erosion, landslides, floods, avalanches, over grazing, uprooting of trees, over-exploitation, etc. The

Forest resources of Kinnaur must be conserved at every cost (Chandra 1992: 46–47). The on-going development activities has posed a great challenge to the bio-diversity and forestry in the district.

Wildlife Sanctuaries

In order to protect, propagate and develop the fast dwindling local flora and fauna, 2 national parks, 3 Ramsar sites and 32 wildlife sanctuaries have been created in Himachal Pradesh. Out of these, three wildlife sanctuaries have been formed in district Kinnaur. These are: (i) Lippa-Asrang Wildlife Sanctuary (ii) Rakchham-Chhitkul Wildlife Sanctuary, and (iii) Rupi-Bhabha Wildlife Sanctuary.

The Lippa-Asrang wildlife sanctuary was first notified a sanctuary in 1962 and re-notified on 27 March 1974. This sanctuary is among the few in Himachal Pradesh which is not open to tourist. There are two villages namely Lippa and Asrang having a human population of about 2,400 and cattle population of 21,921. The alpine pasture is the medicinal storehouse for the local residents. There are hardly any trees in the sanctuary area. Juniper shrubs represent the vegetation. Rakchham-Chhitkul Wildlife Sanctuary: It was first notified in 1962 and re-notified on 27 March 1974. It is located in Baspa or Sangla valley in Kalpa Sub-Division of Tribal Belt of Kinnaur district of the Himachal Pradesh. The vast pastures of this sanctuary act as a storehouse of many medicinal herbs such as Dhoop (*Jurinea macrocephalla*), Karoo (*Gentiana kurroo*), Patish (*Aconitum heterophyllum*), Kuth (*Saussurea lappa*), Banafsha (*Viola canescens*), Kala-Zeera (*Carum carvi*) and Kesar (*Crocus sativus*). The thick forest of Deodar (*Cedrus deodara*), Kail (*Pinus wallichiana*), Fir (*Abies spectabilis*), Spruce (*Picea smithiana*), broad-leaf *Betula* sp. are the characteristics of this area (Balokhra 2008: 82).

Rupi-Bhabha wildlife sanctuary was first notified a sanctuary on 28 March 1982 and re-notified on 30 June 1982. It is situated in Satluj valley and lies in between 77° 50′ to 78° 51′ East longitudes, and 31° 11′ to 32° 40′ North longitudes. The biological, geomorphologic, aesthetic, snow-clad mountains and scenic beauty of Rupi-Bhabha Wildlife Sanctuary combine to make it a tourist paradise and conservation of rare and endangered plants. The forests of *Pinus wallichiana, Cedrus deodara, Abies* and *Picea* with broad leaf patches provide a diversity to vegetation. The broad leaf species mainly include oaks, walnut, horse chestnut, maples, bird cherry, *Betula*, wild poplar and *Pyrus* species. Hydro power projects have become big challenge to the environment in the area. Ecology of the area has been disturbed it is reflected through climatic change, loss of bio-diversity, de-forestation in the area.

Economic Aspects

Kinnauras are primarily an agro-pastoral tribe. Sheep and goat as well as ponies and horses have always played an important role in their economy. In the past they had trade links with the Tibet.

Agriculture

It is still the main source of the livelihood for very vast majority of the people of Kinnaur. Due to fancy profits people are switching over from the traditional crops to high yielding and remunerative cash crops like apples and dried fruits. The farmers are rising off seasonal vegetables like cabbage, peas, tomatoes, beans, seed potato and pulses. Spectacular results have been reported and areas under high yielding varieties of wheat, barley and maize have gone up from 842 hectares to 1,442 hectares. Likewise the area under vegetables and pulses has jumped from 286 to 848 hectares. Altitude determines the time of sowing and reaping of the different crops. Rabi crops are usually sown from the middle of the September to middle of the December and are reaped in April and July in the lower and higher regions respectively. Kharif crops are sown from March to middle of the July and reaped from September to the end of November.

Horticulture

Kinnaur now occupies a place of pride on the horticultural map of the Himachal Pradesh. Climate of the district is cold and dry and ideally suited for the production of temperate fruits which can be dried. District is endowed with excellent climatic and soil conditions for the production of a wide variety of fruits. Apples, apricots, almonds and walnuts are grown all over the district. Peaches, plums, pears, cherry, and hazelnuts are widely grown in Nichar, Kalpa and Moorang areas. Kagzi almonds grown here match the best quality of almonds grown anywhere in India. Grapes are grown in Kalpa, Morang and Ribba. The area under fruit cultivation has been consistently increasing from 560 hectares to 1,742 hectares in last 20 years. The economic condition of the people, as compared to the past has improved. Near about 67 per cent of the families are dependent on agro-horticultural activities in Pooh sub division. Apples have recorded about sixteen times increase in last 15 years, and are mainly responsible for raising the economic status and upliftment of the life-style of the common people.

Animal Husbandry

Livestock husbandry has always played an important role in the economy of this arid and hard region of the state. At present it generates approximately twelve per cent of the total income of the development block. Of the entire livestock population, sheep and goats account for sixty nine per cent. Chief among the domestic animals are horse, mule, donkey, yak, cow, ox, sheep, goat, mare, dog and goat. A horse and mule breeding scheme has been taken up and a farm is located at Jeori (in Shimla district) at the border of the Kinnaur. The breeding programme in this farm is broadly based on the crossing of Spiti and Chamurthi mares with Connemara stallions. Poultry farming has also been taken up with the opening of the farms at Tapri and Reckong Peo. Fisheries Department has made efforts to improve the fishing activity in the district. Now fishing has been brought under a national licensing system. Construction of a new Trout farm at Sangla was undertaken in 1960–61. The objective was to raise sufficient number of fishes every year to provide game to the anglers and the tourists and to the local people. Yak and sheep breeding farms have been established in Karcham and Sangla respectively (Sharda 1998: 209). District Kinnaura has its own distinct identity in the Himachal society. The Kinnauras are known to have a rich heritage. People have strong affinity with their culture. Tribal society in this area is not lagging behind the general population in Himachal. With the corporate activities on the rise, the area is not inaccessible now-a-days. Their economic status has improved considerably but lopsided development activities challenge the Kinnaura tribal identity as well as the eco-system of the area.

Conclusion

Kinnaura tribe of Himachal is one of the most developed tribe of India. It covers the international boundary area adjoining Tibet. This tribe finds its references in the Hindu, Jain and Buddhist literature. Kinnauras have rich cultural heritage. They value their tradition, but are equally conscious of harbouring a progressive outlook. Their social life is associated with traditional institutions and roles. Society is caste based. Power structures and roles have clear influence of the caste institutions. Agro economy in the area is supplemented by the service sector and business activities. Kinnaura being one of the most resourceful districts, is on the top priority of the state and centre developmental proposals. Developmental activities have disturbed the calm and serene human and physical environment of the 'tribal Kinnaur'.

8

Tribal Community and the Local Power Politics

Democracy stands for the mass involvement in the political process. Democracy as a concept includes socio, economic, political, and administrative dimensions. Success of one rests on the others. Imbalance among them defeats the purpose of democracy. In different democratic systems of the world (liberal as well as socialist democracies) masses face different kinds of deprivation due to more emphasis on one dimension of the democracy and ignoring the others. Political democracy is one of the important dimensions of the inclusive democracy. Mass involvement at every level of the governance has become important to make democracy a great success. In case of India it was realised after 45 years of the independence that effective participation of the masses is inevitable to evolve a society projected in the Indian Constitution by our founding fathers. They defined the concept of 'Future India' as a country based on the liberal principles with the aim of providing social justice to the last one in the society. In this field in late fifties of the twentieth century Government of India appointed Balwant Rai Mehta Committee (BRM) The committee focused on the issue of mass participation in the democratic process and suggested ways to strengthen the socio-economic and political democracy in the rural and tribal society of the country. Mehta suggested mass participation through the PRIs Committee recommended community involvement in development activities would streamline the rural Indian society as well as it would help in conditioning the participatory democracy. Further community's role to achieve the goal of good governance is very important. On the lines of the 73rd Amendment 1993, Panchayati Raj extended to the

Kinnaura Tribe of Rarang Village (Kinnour)

Tracking Kinnaura through Chanshal Pass

Scheduled Areas under the PESA Act 1996. Basic objective of these efforts on the part of the government is to involve the tribal communities in the local governance with special efforts to empower them to protect and promote their own practices to manage the local affairs (within the ambit of the Indian Constitution).

Section I
Views of Kinnaura Respondents

Socio-Economic Profile of the Kinnaura Respondents

Kinnaura tribe among the Indian tribes is considered to be one of the most aware and developed tribe. To evaluate the tribal scenario after the implementation of the Panchayati Raj, the chapter is devoted to understand the existing situation of the tribal leadership, their role perception and role performance in the context of the participatory democracy among the Kinnaura tribe. 390 community members were interviewed in the area and their opinion analysed to understand and assess the effectiveness of the PRIs after the implementation of the PESA Act in the area. All the three blocks of the district of Kinnaura have been covered. Issues related to the tribal participation in the Gram Sabha, their satisfaction with PRIs and issues related to the development are being dealt with in this chapter.

District Kinnaur falls in the Scheduled Area under the V Schedule of the Indian Constitution. Majority of the people in Himachal Pradesh live in rural areas, out of that 5.6 per cent which is included in the rural population lives in tribal areas. They are dependent upon agriculture for their livelihood. Farming is the main occupation of people living in the villages of Himachal Pradesh. Apart from the agriculture and horticulture, business, daily wage earning and government jobs are also important economic activities in the Himachal Pradesh in general, particularly in the tribal areas. 67 per cent of the respondents were agriculturist/horticulturist professionals, 16 per cent respondent were from the service sector and 17 per cent were from the business community. Professional profile of Kinnauras also indicate that majority of the working population is engaged in agriculture, horticulture and are traditional artisans. Another important variable which has its bearing on the economic status of the family is its income. It determines the standard of living of a family. Family income here refers to all sources through which members have more returns of their economic activities (Joshi 1994: 34). Nearly 16 per cent of the respondents were having annual income below ₹ 25,000, 26 per cent having annual income below ₹ 50,000, 37 per cent of the respondents were having annual income below ₹ 1 lakh and 21 per cent of the respondents were having annual income of 2 lakh and above. Tribals in Himachal are economically well off as compared to the tribals in others states. Economic dimension of the society is important, class has important role in the power politics. In all the elections (Parliament to village Panchayat), elite section always play an important role. Also, moneyed people have dominance and they are preferred as leaders in their own community. Moneyed people have dominant position in the power system of Kinnaura.

Himachal tribals have a typical caste system. According to K.S. Singh (1985: 71), 'field studies have revealed the infinitely complex formation of Jatis: their ranking differs from place to place; their world view vary. The jatis cannot be strait jacket into the varna scheme; there is no obvious lack between the two. The conceptual framework of *chautrvarna* has been found to be rigid, too 'amorphous' to fit in the social realities of *jatis* which are more dynamic, complex and wide ranging'. In Himachal, tribes theory given by Singh is relevant to some extent. In Lahaul, Pangi and Bharmaur regions, caste system is almost same as in the Hindu society. Majority of the people in the area are migrants from the plains. They have continued with their caste practices with few changes. In Kinnaura tribe, caste division is different from the Hindu caste system of four castes which is in existence in other two tribal pockets. Society is mainly divided into two castes: the upper caste known as *Khoshiya* and lower caste known as *Chomang*. They have one more group known as *Domangs* (artisan class). Latter two are treated as untouchables. Within the untouchables also there is a difference of untouchability. Domangs can enter in the houses of the Khoshiyas but they do not share food with them. Chomangs are totally untouchables. Khoshiyas do not have any kind of the social interaction with them. They have their own customary norms to conduct the caste practices within their society. Khoshiyas enjoy higher status as compared to the Domangs and Chomangs. Broadly on the basis of the professional classification *Khoshiyas* are land-owning class of the society and Domangs and *Chomangs* are service providers in different fields. They are iron smith, gold smith, leather workers and also the people who play musical instruments (Bajantris). All these services are indispensable for the Kinnauras, still this section is treated as untouchable by the Khoshiyas. Both the sections obey the customary laws in regulating their behaviour in the society and the lower caste people harbour no grudges against the upper caste behaviour towards them. This is the accepted behaviour pattern of the Kinnaura society. Kinnaur stratification system qualifies the Singh's thesis (1985: 75) Clan exogamy and tribe Jati endogamy are generally characteristics of settled, large and homogenous communities. There is no evidence that these institutions were borrowed from Brahmins.

Economic and political system is also caste driven in the Kinnaura society. Economically Khoshiyas belong to the elite class. They are land lords having large orchards. After the corporate activities in the area, land owning class benefitted substantially by the land acquisition in the area. It has added to their better financial position. Some of them entered in the business activities, started transportation business and contractor ship. The service class (Domangs and Chomangs) suffered economically. They used to earn their living by practising traditional occupations and working on the land of land lords. Most of the tribal have land holdings but lower castes have small holdings or patta. Land acquisition and the corporate activities did not prove beneficial to the unskilled labour in the area. Their livelihood prior to the projects was dependent on the multiple petty economic activities. The corporate world and its activities added to their problems. They are not able to compete with the skilled labour of plains. With the effect of the liberalisation and globalisation locals developed their taste for those goods and services which are available in the market. They lost taste for the local products. Traditional economy in the tribal area is in a pathetic condition. In the local politics *Khoshiyas* have an effective political participation as compared to the *Domangs* and *Chomangs*. Formal power structures are dominated by the *Khoshiyas*. Lower caste people are manoeuvre by the *Khoshiyas* in the local institutions also.

Personal information, age, education, marital status, family structure together helps to understand the socio-cultural set up of the society as well as its orientation towards the political institutions. Out of all, 18 per cent respondents were in the age group between 18–30, 29 per cent between 30–40, maximum 32 per cent in the age group between 40–50 and 21 per cent above fifty years. Age profile of the respondents indicates middle age respondents were the most enthusiastic in their responses. They have time for community service. Other important variable that affects power structure and roles is gender. Gender stands for the perception and role assignment to the male and female according to specific societal culture. The male and female have specific roles; rearing the children, taking care of the family are the perceived and assigned role of the women in the Indian society, whereas outdoor activities are considered to be in the domain of male folk. Irrespective of the area in all parts of the country, roles are defined by keeping the gender variable in mind. With the passage of time, women are trying to locate themselves in a better position as active members of the community. Although women are marginalised in the political arena, the women respondents were more as compared to their male counter parts. Women community is more active as voters, a fact that is illustrated by the electoral data of the last two decades. Women voter turnout has considerably increased in the elections from the national level to the local bodies in all the states. Fifty per cent reservation in the 2015 PRIs elections gave momentum to the women empowerment in the local politics. Women try to cash in on every opportunity in order to express themselves. Same trend is visible among the tribal women elsewhere. On the basis of the study conducted in tribal areas of Odisha (Singh 2015: 543–549) they inferred 'Women are there in all the three tiers of the Panchayati Raj system. Women conceptualise governance as the process for the implementation of government sponsored schemes aimed at poverty reduction and infra-structure building. Recently these women have witnessed a great change in the women's life and the government has started focusing attention on empowerment of women also'.

With the constitutional status to the PRIs, these institutions have become effective institutions. Their organisation, perception and the seriousness of the society is reflected through composition of the PRIs. Rural society demands lettered leadership; education has become an important qualification for acquiring leadership in modern society. Generally, in the rural areas, an educated person is highly regarded (Sharma 1994: 262). Out of total respondents only 7 per cent were illiterate, 9 per cent were having educational level up to the primary, 22 per cent up to middle, 28 per cent were having qualification up to matriculation and 18 per cent passed 10+2, 11 per cent were graduates, 5 per cent were post graduates. Amidst the tribals, mainstream education is considered to be important for the personal and over all development of the society. Educated people are more active in the social and political life. At least 93 per cent people are at the working literacy stage. They can understand and respond as the Gram Sabha members in the meetings. Marriage as an institution in the Indian society brings considerable changes in one's life. Social life is also determined by marital status. Everybody gets more involved in the family life after marriage. In addition to the superior role, women particularly get freedom for social interaction. 64 per cent of the respondents were married and the rest were the unmarried. In general, mainstream women are less open and take less part in the social and political activities, especially the unmarried women. In the tribal society it is observed that women enjoy more freedom as they have less social constraints as compared to the common women of the Indian society. Nathan's (1994) thesis that tribal societies are more open and egalitarian qualifies the Kinnaura society where women enjoy social freedom. Numerical data suggests higher number of married respondents is an evidence that the younger age groups may be more involved in their personal affairs in the tribal society and they do not find time for social and political life. Women in the area are not much enthusiastic to join the power game in the society. Their political aspirations, to be part of the rural power structures, are not very high. Their participation is confined to vote and attend the Gram Sabha meetings according to their interest and convenience. Existing trend indicates that they are interested in the basic political participation by being members of the community. They may not be ready at present to wear the responsibility of leadership.

Empirical Assessment of the PESA Act (1996)

PESA provides extensive powers to the tribal communities to manage their affairs according to their own system within the purview of the Indian Constitution. Under the PESA Act, Gram Sabha can use its powers effectively to resolve the tribal issues regarding the Land Acquisition, Minor Forest Product (MFP) and protection of the ecological balance in the remote areas. In the era of the open economies it is one of the most important issues to make the tribal community of the country aware and intact their society from the non-tribals. Empowerment in the above fields has great importance for them. More than 2/3rd (59 female, 22 male) respondents were not aware of the PESA. Inference on the basis of the response is that the tribals have little knowledge about the government initiatives, in form of the PESA Act 1996. It can cause misutilisation of the powers by the PRIs and local bureaucracy.

Gram Sabha is the legislative organ of the village Panchayat. Ideally this institution is the most effective media of direct democracy. In Millennium Goals of the UNO, 'good governance' is an important issue. It stands mainly for the mass participation in the decision-making, accountability and transparency. Gram Sabha can strengthen the process of good governance. Periodical meetings of the Gram Sabha to deliberate on the development issues, to audit the Panchayat's function can be fruitful if the institution perform its duties religiously and people have faith in its efficacy. When the people were asked about the role of Gram Sabha in the development activities, 75 per cent people responded in positive manner, 7 per cent had negative view and 18 per cent had no opinion. During the field work it was observed that only few people were active in the Gram Sabha meetings, rest were mere spectators. There was effective numerical strength but people had little communication in the meeting. Either they were friends or family members of the Panchayat leaders, or they attended the meeting under the pressure of the leaders. If the participation will be effective it will be a landmark step in the process of the participatory democracy. Participation is a wide term that comprises involvement. Participation here is a process through which people directly participate in the decision-making, implementation and evaluation at the grassroots level. Nearly 50 per cent of the respondents affirmed that they participated in the Gram Sabha, 36 per cent respondents responded vis-à-vis and 14 per cent rendered no opinion. During the meetings of the Gram Sabha they generally discussed development issues (construction of community hall, construction of PHC, construction of Bus Stand, initiative regarding employment generation programmes, awareness about PESA Act, awareness about Forest Right Act, creating opportunities for agriculture produce, expansion of pasture land, renovation of *anganwadi* in the locality, review of the budgets, selection of beneficiaries, sanitation and identification of IRDP families for development programmes). Gram Sabha proceedings indicate community orientation towards the development. It is observed that the people are not aware about the legal and technical provisions. Their main thrust is on the development issues in the areas.

Conclusion

In the tribal Kinnaur after the implementation of PESA Act 1996, gradual changes are taking place. Reservation for the marginalised section provided opportunities to the women and SC in the tribal community. Social change is gradual, its impact is visible in the role performance of the local institutions. Patriarchy, caste and class have strong influence on leadership psyche of area. Discussion in the Gram Sabha mainly revolves around developmental issues and it reflects their concerns, although they have meagre knowledge regarding the procedural aspect of the local governance. Tribal women are satisfied with their social and economic empowerment and by nature they have little interest in garnering political power.

9

Tribal Pocket of Lahaul and Spiti in Himachal Pradesh

Lahaulas

Lahaulas reside in Lahaul. It is one of the remotest areas of the state. Lahaul is enclosed by high mountains from all the sides and is accessible from outside only through difficult and dangerous passes. Its climate is dry and cold; vegetation is scanty; and arable land is extremely limited. Moreover, it is impossible to grow anything without water, and only one crop is sown in a year (Gill 1972: 21).

Lahaul with the area of about 2,000 square miles is situated between north latitude 30°8′ and 32°59′ and east longitude 76°30′ and 77°50′. Surroundings include Rubsha and Zanskar on the North; Kullu and Banghal on the south; Spiti on the East; and Chamba on the West. Shape of the tract is roughly rectangular with the Greater Himalaya on the north and mid Himalaya on the south end on the east and west. Mean relaxation of these hills is 18,000 and that of its inhabited parts is about 9,000 above sea level (Tobdan 1984: 1)

In the lap of the Himalayas in the North Western corner of India, there exists a small valley called Lahaul. Word Lahaul presumably is composed of two Tibetian words: Lah+Yul. Lah means 'god' and yul means 'the land'. Lahaul means 'the land of gods, or the abode of gods'. It is a very narrow valley, or in fact a collection of three separate valleys formed roughly in a 'y' shape. In the east the river Chandra forms the right branch of the 'y'. This valley is called the Chandra valley, which includes Gondhla and Rangla area. Bhaga River forms the left branch, and is called the Bhaga valley, constituted of the Gahar and Tod valleys.

Together they become Chandra-Bhaga, forming the lower stem of the 'y' including the Pattan valley and the Chamba Lahaul area, also known as Goonam. Average width of each of these valleys is barely a couple of nautical miles of the populated area and another fifty nautical miles of barren mountain slopes. Valley of the Lahaul is surrounded by the districts of Kangra and Kullu in the south, the valleys of Spiti and Kinnaur to the east, Ladakh and Zanskar to the north, and Chamba and Kishtwar to the West (Sahni 1994: 18).

The Lahaulas inhabit the Chandra and Bhaga valleys from Rohtang La to Baralacha and Sisu to Kungan La. They belong to two geographical zones. The first is the Pattan valley and the Lahulas here are more Aryan than Mongoloid. The second is the Gahal valley and the Lahulas here tend to be more Mongoloid than Aryan (Basu 1985: 54).

Lahaul, over the course of time, turned out to be a meeting ground for different races-Aryan, Mongoloid and Dravidian. Language runs into four streams. Tibetan is spoken in Keylong, Bhaga valley, Koksar and Chandra valley, and in the entire Gahar area. Boonum is spoken in Goomerang Kothee, Kardung Kothee and Barbok Kothee. Manchat (Pattan), which is mostly Hindi mixed with a little Tibetian, spoken in Tandee, Warpa, Rance-Kam Yanampet (Yampeeo, Jobran, Goee, Teenu – which has Tibetian words and a sprinkling of Manchat, Boonum, Hindi and Persian words, is spoken in Goudhla and Chandra valley. Lahaula is a term to describe the people who normally reside in Lahaul after the carving of district Lahaul and Spiti. Collectively, the term is used to describe the people of this district. In Lahaul Swangla, Khampas and Bodh sub tribals resides. Swangla is a scheduled tribe living in the Pattan valley tract along with river Chandra Bhaga in district Lahaul and Spiti. They are Rajput and Brahmins. The languages spoken by them are Manchhad (mixture of Tibetian and Hindi), Chinnali (spoken by the Lohar), Bhoti (spoken by Bodhs) and Tinan or Tinent (spoken by people of Sisu area. Swanglas resembles the Munda speaking tribe of Bihar, Bengal and Central Asia. Lingua Franca of the area confirms that the people in the area have their origin in the plains of central India and they had close association with the Tibet. Khampas and Bodhs have their association with Tibetian culture, social practices and religious moorings. Swanglas' caste practices and stratification system resembles to the Hindu practices.

Marriage practices in Swanglas (i) *Rusta-te Byah*: Marriage by elopement (where a girl and boy fall in love with each other and marry), (ii) *Kua-Byah*: Marriage by capture by boy, (iii) *Mazmi-Byah*: Boy sends his sister to bring the girl as he himself finds unable to bear the marriage expenses. People follow them according to their convenience. Divorce is also a part of the Swangla social system: the couple who wants to be separated holds the thread that symbolises the breaking of matrimonial.

Khampa is the other tribal group in Lahaul. They are believed to have migrated from Tibet. It is an entrepreneur community who are engaged in trade. In Spiti they are known by the name 'Piti Khampa', and in Lahaul as 'Gharja Khampa'. The dialect spoken by them is known as Khampa. Their marriages are generally fixed by negotiator known as Phakhtum. Divorce among Khampas is known as *Jatsari-jha-dal-va* or *Jha-cho-che*. They follow the Buddhism four sects of Lamaistic Buddhism. Traditional council of Khampas is known as Shuzam Chungi headed by Gova.

The Lahaulas grow cash crops like potatoes, kuth and hops. They also cultivate wheat, barley, maize, vegetables, buckwheat and pulses. Their food habits are simple. They are good at animal husbandry and produce milk, butter, ghee and cheese. Many Lahulas have orchards in Kullu valley. Some are highly educated-overall literacy level being 77.24 per cent (Census 2011).

District of Lahaul-spiti is a unique sociological unit in one of the frontier districts of India in Himachal Pradesh. It is a barren, desolate and wind-swept region and lies at an average elevation of over 3,500 mt. People of Lahaul are of mixed race. They are mainly Buddhists and their dialect resembles the Tibetian dialect. According to Hutchison and Vogels (quoted in Chauhan 1998: 204), Buddhism spread in the area on the initiative of translator Lochen Rinchen Zanpo in the 10th century AD. Key Monastery was founded in 14th century. Buddhism and Hinduism are two main religions followed by the Lahauals. Lahauls are tough, honest, hospitable, hardworking and healthy. Their economy is basically supplemented by weaving, spinning; while the modern generation is engaged in tourism and hydro-power projects in the area. With the liberalisation, outside economic activities have influenced the Lahaula economy and society. People of the area are not happy with the changing economic contours and excessive use of the natural resources in the tribal belt.

Caste system is prevalent among Lahaulas. Their caste system, traditions and social structure is akin to the Pangwals. The Lahaulas who inhabit both Lahaul and Spiti region is divided into two major categories. The upper caste consists of Rajputs, Brahmins, Thakurs and Rathis, while the lower caste includes Halis, Bhots and Lohars. In Himachal tribes, caste pattern vary in three tribal areas.'Caste and class society do not suddenly spring into existence when clearly formed classes and castes appear on historical scene' (Nathan 1994: 5). In Lahaul upper caste consists of many sub-castes but in Kinnaur there are no sub-castes. Upper caste is known as Khoshiyas in Kinnaur. Caste groups are endogamous. People strictly follow customary laws in the context of the caste system. Lahualas are mainly Thakurs and Brahmins. Thakurs who comprise the gentry and the titular rulers of Lahaul are of Tibetan origin. They take Kanet women as concubines but not as legally wedded wives.

The sons of such unions are not considered pure Thakurs, but after few generations assert their Thakur origin. Brahmins of Lahaul marry Kanet women, and their sons have right to succession, though the father will not eat from such sons' hands. The sons born from such marriages are called 'gurus' and they in turn may marry Kanet women or those of mixed caste. They wear white or brown coloured kattar (a long loose Tibetan gown), while younger generation wears coat. Tobri (Kullu cap) is a common head gear and suthan (warm tight trousers) is used to cover the lower parts of the body (legs). Lahauli women adorn their dress with ornaments on the head and neck to look more attractive. Lahaulas are mostly non-vegetarians and do not consider any food or drink as taboo. Lugri is the local name for a drink. Matrimonial alliances are mainly arranged, they are not monogamous but polyandrous.

Spiti

People of the Spiti bear unmistakable evidences on their faces of their Chinese or Mongolian descent. Men are stout, well-built fellows, and the women are also very strongly framed (Harcourt 1972: 43). Spiti lies between North latitude 31°42′ and 32°58′ and east longitude 77°21′ and 78°35′; its area is 2,155 square miles. It may be well to note that although the name Spiti is spelt in the vernacular as in English, initial S in elided and the word is pronounced 'piti' (Verma 1997: 1).

Spiti is completely hemmed in by lofty mountain ranges at an average elevation of 18,000 feet or more above the sea, which divide from Waziri inner Saray of the Plach tehsil and from Waziris Rupi and Lahaul of the Kullu tehsil on the west, from Rampur-Bushahr state on the south, from great Tibet on the east and from Ladakh on the north. It consists of the upper valley of the Spiti river which, rising from the western Himalaya at an elevation from the western Himalaya about 16,000 feet and at a point not far away from the source of the Chenab, a south eastern course, leaving the Waziri by a gorge cut through the mountain range to the east, and thereafter flowing through Rampur-Bushahr state to join the Sutlej. End of the river at the point where it escapes from Spiti, the lowest part of the Waziri, is about 11,000 feet from the sea level. Northern slopes of the range which form the watershed of the Spiti River to the north are also considered as included in the Waziri, forming a strip of uninhabited alpine waste extending from the boundary of Tibet on the east to the Lingti plain, a similar strip of territory attached to Waziri. Lahaul on the west of the Serchhu stream, whose waters ultimately find their way to the Indus, being generally regarded as the boundary between Spiti and Lahaul in the direction (Agnew 1899: 71).

Literally the name Spiti means 'middle land' is so called because it is surrounded by mountain ranges on all sides. It also lies between major former empires of Bushahr, Kullu, Ladakh and Tibet. Spiti is linked with Lahaul administratively. This district of Himachal Pradesh is called as 'Lahaul and Spiti district' and the Commissioner's office is at Keylong, in Lahaul. An Assistant District Commissioner looks after the affairs of Spiti. For administrative convenience, Spiti extends southwards along the course of the Parchu, across the Parang la forming an internal boundary with Ladakh, though geographically this area should be in Ladakh. From the west of Sumdo, the point where the Parchu meets the Spiti river, is considered the area of the Spiti, forming its border with Kinnaur (Bajpai 1987: 25).

Spiti sub-division is more barren and difficult to traverse than Lahaul sub-division. Spiti is bound by mountain ranges of the great and the middle Himalaya on all sides, with average elevation of the valley floor being 4,270 mt. Last mountain ranges are pierced in the southeast by the narrow gorge of the Spiti river as it rushes out to meet the Satluj. Western boundary is about 128 kilometres long and is bounded on the north by the Kunzum range. It runs south, dividing the border of the Spitii with Kullu valleys (of the Parvati) and meets the Srikand range of the Kinnaur. On the east the range starts at Parangla and runs along the crest of the Himalaya dividing Tibet with India. It has two major breaks, one near Kaurik where the Parchu re-enters Indian territory and finally at khab where the Satluj enters India.

The entire terrain is dry with an annual rainfall of about 17 cm. Thus Spiti is a typical mountain desert with bare mountain sides. Such dry weather makes it favourable for o trek all through summer. These factors are now changing though, the Spiti or the Trans Himalayan weather is not so dry and arid (Kapadia 1996: 26–27).

Khampas

Khampas are the nomadic tribe which has organised trade along the Himalayan borders. After 1962 they started settlements in Lahaul, Spiti, Ladakh, Kullu, Kinnaur, Bushahr, Mandi and Kangra. Their houses stand out as they have Buddhist flags flying from the roofs They are a fine Tibetan race. Khampas engaged themselves in trading various commodities and wandered from place to place in India and Tibet, hawking their merchandise, accompanied by their beasts of burden (mostly ponies). With the disruption of access to Tibet after Chinese occupation and the advent of vehicular traffic they have progressively switched to settled life. Khampas have intermingled with the Aryans and other Central Asian racial groups. Women have long and thick hair and a fine face, sharp nose, thin lips and deep set eyes. Colonies of the Khampas used to be a common site in April/May and October/November on the banks of the Beas in the Kullu valley. In fact, in summer they move to the Himalayan frontiers and in winter descend with their products for sale. Khampas have never reared sheep, goats or yaks, but they kept horses, ponies, dogs and asses for transporting their goods. Many Ladakhis, Lahaulis and Pitials have married their women and the Khampa males, in turn, have married Ladakhi, Lahauli and Pitial women. A marriage traditionally is by 'capture'. A lavish feast is offered in which meat and drinks are generously served. The Khampas are generally monogamous but instances of polygamy are also been recorded.

The Shiar Khampas are those dealing in trade along the border. They are also known as the Mekhore Khampas and come to India to visit religious places. The Piti Khampas live in Spiti as nomads. The Garja Khampas belong to Lahaul and are nomads. The Khunu Khampas live in Rampur Bushahr and are also nomads. Some Khampas are now engaged in agriculture, horticulture, animal husbandry and government jobs (Panchani 1994: 83).

Swangla

Swangla is a scheduled tribe exclusively living in the Pattan valley track along the Chandra Bhaga in Lahaul-Spiti district. Like some other tribes Swangla is a generic term, which includes both Brahmin and Rajput. Different theories have been given about the origin of the Swanglas. According to the legend, when Taimur invaded this part of the country he drove the Buddhists out and occupied the territory and the people came to be known as Swangla from 'Swanl', earlier name of the area. Another version considers them immigrants from Chamba, displaying Mediterranean features. This conjecture can be possible justification in the light of Chamba being adjacent district to Lahaul-Spiti. According to yet another theory, these people have originally migrated from Sangla Valley in the Kinnaur, which was subjected to Tibetan subjugation. Swanglas are presently living wholly in this trace of the Lahaul-Spiti (Balokhra 2008: 69).

Jads

Most of the Jads are agriculturists, while others do business of wool. They are polyandrous and patrilineal tribe. In Jads unmarried girls are known as Jamos (the chronic bachelor).

Conclusion

Lahaul and Spiti district Himachal Pradesh is tribal area. People who reside in this area known as Jahauls. Within tribal community of Lahaulas there are many sub-groups. They are endogamous group having their district cultural practices.

10

Tribals of Bharmour and Pangi

Pangwals

Pangwals live in the Pangi area of the Chamba district in the Chandra Bhaga valley. They are not pure Mongoloids but have some Aryan traces in them. They have emigrated from various parts of the hills, especially from the Lahaul and Kullu, Ravi valley and Chinab. Geographical seclusion for centuries can be one of the causes of their conservative nature in their beliefs and customs. They follow the caste system the castes being Brahmins, Rajputs, Thakurs, Rathis, Malis, Lohars, Moghs and Dakis. They adhere to some religious practices such as temples dedicated to Devi, Nag and Siva. Principal Devi temple is at Mindhal. People are backward (Panchani 1994: 78). They are primarily agriculturist but also rear sheep and goats. Livestock has important role in their lifestyle. Marriage is an important institution in their social set up. Divorce among them is easy. Inheritance is in the male line. Normally, monogamy is followed and widow marriage is also not considered taboo in this society.

Pangi, administrative subdivision of the Chamba district is a forlorn world. Time and space acquire a new dimension in this snowbound, land-locked, narrow valley sandwiched between mighty Pir-panjal and Zanskar ranges of the Himalaya. It is located in the mid-Himalayan region known as Pangi range spread between north latitude 32°11′30″ and 33°13′06″ and east longitude 75°45′ and 77°03′33″.

Pangi range is in direct continuation of the Himalayan axis which separates Kullu district of Himachal Pradesh from Lahaul and Spiti district, and enters Chamba's boundary on the western border of the Bara Bangahal region of the Kangra district. It then passes through

Chamba from south-east to north-west for about 130 km in its journey into two large but unequal parts, northern or smaller part was called Pangi and Chamba-Lahaul, and the other part was called British Lahaul. Due to this natural partition these two regions are separated from each other and there is no communication between the two during the larger part of the year. Even in the summers when the movement is possible it is very difficult to interact with each other.

Pangi and Chamba-Lahaul which were part of the erstwhile Chamba State are two distinct administrative units now. While Pangi is a sub division of Chamba district, Chamba-Lahaul which is known as Udaipur is a subdivision of Lahaul and Spiti district. Pangi valley remains cut off from the rest of the world for about six months in a year. Heavy snowfall and semi-arctic conditions makes living very tough in the valley (Chaudhry 2002: 1).

Pangi is unique in its grandeur and beauty; surpassing any other part of the district. The scenery is sublime and imposing. 'Nature appears in her wildest and grandest moods. Everything is on a stupendous scale. The great river rolls along in a deep and narrow gorge, lashing itself into fury against the adamantine cliffs that confine it. Precipice spring from the brink in places almost perpendicular to a height of one to two thousand feet: on the lower ranges are grassy slopes of rich pasture with dense forests of pine and cedar, while high over all, the stern and majestic mountains, piled on one another, attain an attitude of 18,000 to 21,000 feet rising far beyond the line of eternal snow'. But all is not rugged sublimity and naked grandeur. At every few miles, the traveller reaches fairly open nooks of surpassing beauty, which may have been small lakes in some by-gone age, while the river was cutting its way through a rocky barrier in front. There are a few villages. They are chiefly met in the sub-valleys'.

There are several beautiful side valleys in Pangi, the principle being Sural, Hundan, Saichu and Parmar, all leading upto the Zanskar Range. Though narrow where they join the main valley, they are fairly open higher up and between them contain a considerable number of villages. Those near the head of each Nala are occupied by people marked by Mongolian features. They are called Bhot, and their villages Bhotori (Verma 1996: 5–6).

Gaddis

Gaddis are people found in certain areas of Himachal Pradesh and Punjab. They are also found in Kashmir. In Himachal, Bharmour sub-tehsil of the Chamba district is also called 'Gadderan', the home land of Gaddi. It is from here that this tribal population has, down the generations, spilt over certain other parts of the district and even to some other areas of the Himachal Pradesh. In pre-British days, therefore, their villages and cultivated lands fell within the jurisdiction of the two states of Chamba and Kangra. Many of them, in fact, cultivated wheat as a crop in Kangra and crossed over the snow ranges in summer to cultivate another crop in Bharmour. In the Bharmour sub-tehsil and in the other parts of the Chamba district, Gaddis are divided into four castes: (i) Brahmins (ii) Khatris and Rajputs who regularly wear the sacred thread (iii) Thakur and Rathis who as a rule do not wear it, and (iv) the last class, comprising Kolis, Rihars, Lohars, Baddies, Sipis and Halis (Negi 1976: 137; Singh 1994: 269). Caste as an institution, and its practices were the result of the community's economic pursuits and their interaction with the villagers with whom they used to interact during the economic activities. The association of the Gaddis with the permanent villages and settled agriculture replicate the caste system of the neighbouring societies. Some of the Brahminical *gotras* divisions and migrations myths are also part of Gaddi oral tradition. The Gaddis originally migrated from the plains. The Chauhans, Rajputs and Brahmin Gaddis accompanied by Raja Ajai Verma in 850–870 AD, while Chauham, Harkans, Pakhru, Chiledi, Manglu and Kundali Rajputs, and the Khatris fled to the hills to escape Aurangzeb's persecution.

Most of the Gaddi population is concentrated in Chamba and Bharmour where they have homes. The snowbound Gadderan (where many of them live) at an altitude ranging between 4,000 to 8,000 feet, remain cut off from the rest of the world due to heavy snow and avalanches. Gaddis are believed to have migrated to Bharmour following the suppression of the Rajputs by the Mughals. Circumstances forced them to flee and seek asylum in the hills of the Himachal Pradesh. Wandering in the wilderness, they came upon a place called Bharmour, also called Brahmapura, and chose it as a peaceful, permanent abode for themselves.

Physically, Gaddis are of medium height and have a lot of stamina. Their noses are sharp, colour fair, hair generally black. Gaddi women are also physically very strong, slim and good looking. Both sexes display an alpine character in their facial features. Gaddi house is generally a double storied structure with a verandah on all the sides. Roof is slanted with gables and is made of irregular slate tiles. Stone and wood are the main materials used in the construction of the house. Food of the Gaddis consists of rice, maize, wheat, millet, vegetables and pulses. They are very good agriculturists and grow variety of crops. They are also fond of drinking particularly a local rice, bran and stew (a concoction of several herbs). Common professions of the community are animal rearing, agriculture, small trade, labour, tailoring, carpentry, etc. Gaddis who inhabit mainly Bharmour are semi nomadic. Pastoral Gaddis have pasture rights in Lahaul, Spiti, Kullu and Manali. These rights are hereditary. In the olden times they used to pay a rent to the village head (Thakur or Rana). But after Lyall's settlement report, the rent came to be considered as a state right and the shepherds came to be regarded as tenants of the state. At present, most of the Gaddis are settled on the outskirts of Bharmour, at places like Dharmasala, Palampur, Sihunta, Shahapur, Nurpur and also in the districts of Hamirpur and Mandi (Verma 1996: 48).

Gujjars

Gujjars are nomadic tribe, mostly pastoral. They fall in Hindu as well as in the Muslim communities. They are originally from Afghanistan, North West Frontier province (NWFP) and Kashmir. They rear buffaloes and sell their milk products to earn their livelihood. They live in jungles, villages, valleys for a temporary period and then move further to some other places in search of fodder for their cattle. During summers they are seen in high pastures, while in winters they move to the plains.

There are two kinds of Gujjars, viz. the resident Gujjar who owns fields and a house, and pasture his herd in the neighbouring waste, and the forest Gujjar, who has no land or fixed home and moves with his herd, spending his summer in a shed on the high ranges and winters in the woody parts of the lower hills. The nomadic Gujjars are exclusively a pastoral tribe. They live on the fringe of forests and maintain their existence by the sale of milk, ghee other produce of their herds. Their wealth consists of buffaloes, as that of Gaddis' consists chiefly of sheep and goats. They are pre-dominantly Muslim by faith: Hindu Gujjars found mostly in the districts of Mandi, Kangra, Sirmour, Solan and Bilaspur have now settled down and taken to farming. Gujjars occupy the area between the Jhelum in the west and the Ganges in the east. They inhabit Jammu and Kashmir, lower hills of the Chamba and Kishtwar, sub-hills and valley of Kangra, Mandi, Bilaspur, Solan and the Kumaoun hills. There are divergent views about the origin and migration of this tribe. According to the one view, Gujjar on the father's side was a Rajput but the mother could have hailed from other tribes. Some consider them to have originated from Gujarat and others believe that they come from Gujranwala in west Punjab. The important Gujjar clans are Chauhans, Roas, Katari, Barkat, Khari, Chechi, Koli, Mirs, Khaus, Mehar, and Muhamnads. Their dialect is akin to Rajasthani. In fact, the Gujjar language is not very different from Pahari and there appears to be a common origin. Gujjars of Churaha and Pangi reveal features pointing to a relation with the Tokharins. Most of the Gujjars of the Himalayas are the immigrant Muslims from the plains (Singh 1998: 331).

Gujjars are tall, having strong legs and arms, with well-developed shoulders. They have high cheekbones and full beards. They have sharp features. Women are well built and generally fair skinned. A Gujjar house may have one or two floors. In case it is a double storeyed, it is a permanent settlement. They only have a single storeyed structure in the case of a non-permanent settlement. The material used in construction is stone, mud, plaster and wood.

Gujjars eat rice, wheat, and maize and supplement these with vegetables, butter, butter milk and other milk products. They also eat meat. They are mainly agriculturists and pastoralists though a few are engaged in trade. Nowadays, many are engaged in professions like tailoring, carpentry, shop keeping and jobs. Among Gujjars, monogamy is the general rule. Child marriages are very common. Joint family system is prevalent in this community. Inheritance is on a patrilineal basis. Daughters are generally gifted ornaments and clothes from their parents' side. A widow on remarrying losses her right to the husband's property. Marriage between all cousins is possible (Panchani 1994: 58–59).

To the Gujjars, nomadism is a way of life. They are used to this type of life since time immemorial because of the compulsion of their profession. As a consequence of the changing conditions, Gujjars are a bewildered community and they are in a dilemma because nomadism is under strain and prospects of settled life offer them no satisfaction. Three fourths of the migratory Gujjars belong to Chamba district alone. A large chunk of Gujjars in Himachal Pradesh during winter migrate to the areas of Pathankot, Gurdaspur, Batala, Amritsar, and Hoshiarpur in Punjab and Dehradun and Saharanpur in Uttarakhand and Uttar Pradesh (Attri 2010: 352).

11

PESA Act and Tribal Politics in Himachal Pradesh

Seventy Third Amendment of the Indian Constitution is the landmark development in the field of the rural local government. The amendment is a benchmark measure towards strengthening of the democracy. It recognises the right of the masses to be a part of the decision-making process at the grassroots level. On the lines of the Amendment, PESA Act 1996 has been enacted for the Scheduled Areas under the Fifth Schedule of the Indian Constitution. This Act was framed in conformity with traditional tribal self-rule, by entrusting extraordinary power to Gram Sabha which is not laid down in the national framework of Panchayati Raj Institutions (PRIs). Scheduled areas are hard areas. People in these areas face numerous challenges, including physical as well as manmade. They are far behind on the scale of the development as compared to the general masses in the country. 'The habitat of the tribal communities is in hills, forest and other inaccessible tracts. They have been living by and large in abject poverty. The age old socio-cultural handicaps along with the environmental factors have been significant reasons for lowering their living standard and resulting in subsistence economy. They have been exploited by non-tribal landlords, businessmen, money lenders, and petty officials, etc. who came in contact with them. New PRI system under the PESA Act, 1996 can facilitate the process of democratisation and can protect and promote the rich culture of the tribal societies. It is one of the most powerful Act which recognises the rights of tribal communities for self-rule and their rights on the natural resources in their locality. Keeping in mind this perspective with regards to the Fifth Schedule Areas, under Article

243(M) of the Constitution of India, on the recommendations of Daleep Singh Bhuria Committee, the provision of the Panchayats Extension to the Scheduled Areas (PESA) was enacted by the Parliament in 1996. PESA Act, 1996 is one of the most progressive legislations for tribal regions for self-governance and traditional rights of tribal communities over their natural resources (Hazara 2011: 29–30). The foremost and significant aspect of the Amendment package is the recognition of the need of safeguarding and preserving the traditions and customs of the tribal people/communities, their cultural identities as well as their customary modes of social-personal relations, including the customary modes of resolution of personal/community disputes.

Provision of the PESA Act is a middle path to synthesise the tradition and modernity. It provides wide power to the Gram Sabha over the natural resources in their area. PRIs have also been empowered to manage their affairs in the locality according to their customs and practices. It also provides space to the marginalised sections of the society (reservation to the deprived section) who always remained deprived due to the socio-cultural structures and practices prevailing in their societies. These societies are also heavily loaded with the burden of those institutions and roles which are not compatible to the present and future society based on the democratic principles of equality, liberty and fraternity. Provision of the Act provides opportunity to frame new institutions based on the democratic ethos (formation of new PRIS, empowerment of Gram Sabha) and de-construct age old institutions (patriarchy, gender bias) which were alibis for exploiting the deprived sections in these societies. The Constitution provides opportunities to preserve, protect, and promote their culture in accordance with the provisions enshrined therein. PESA is also relevant for putting those ill practices to an end which stands as a hindrance to the ideals of social justice, equality, liberty and fraternity.

PESA Act is an act that provides safeguard for the protection of tribal life. Many provisions have been conceived to provide teeth to the Act. Governor of the state enjoy extra-ordinary power as the sole custodian of the legislation in the scheduled areas. The governor is empowered to amend any existing law which is contradictory to the provisions of the PESA Act. Gram Sabha is an institution in which the adults of the village have direct participation endowed with extra ordinary powers. Gram Sabha under the PESA enjoys wide powers in managing its affairs and giving concrete shape to the development activities in the area. It is empowered by the Act to function as an institution of self-governance. State legislatures have been made responsible to ensure that the gram sabha and panchayat at the appropriate level are endowed specifically with such powers. In the purview of the gram sabha, the subjects are:

1. Prevention of land alienation,
2. Management of village markets,
3. Imposition of prohibition on certain issue,
4. Having ownership on non-timber forest produce,
5. Exercising control over money lending,
6. Exercising control over institutions and functionaries in all social sectors, and,
7. Having control over local plans and resources.

These subjects have prominent importance from the perspective of the tribal society. Jurisdiction enhances their democratic powers to realise the dream of consolidation of the tribal society within the Constitutional framework. Section 4 of the PESA Act prohibits the state legislature to enact any law which is not compatible to the Act laid down by the centre. The Act is based on the principle of the subsidiarity. Panchayat at the higher level are not supposed to assume powers and authority of any Panchayat at the lower level. Those powers, functions and responsibilities which have been given to the Gram Sabha and Panchayats under the PESA Act.

Mandatory Powers to the Gram Sabha

Tribal communities were always exploited by the non-tribals. Structured efforts in this field were made by the Britishers with Forest Act 1894 and 1927. After independence, government efforts to strengthen and promote the tribal community lacked the participatory approach. Mandatory functions and responsibilities of the Gram Sabha strengthen the participatory democracy and empower the community to protect its interest in the era of liberalisation, privatisation, and globalisation. (i) Before taking up any plan, programme or project for implementation, Gram Panchayat has to take approval from the Gram Sabha. (ii) Gram Sabha is authorised for identification of beneficiaries of poverty alleviation and other programmes and issuance of utilisation of funds by the Gram Panchayat for the above programmes. Planning and management of minor water bodies can be undertaken by Panchayat after getting approval from the Gram Sabha. These powers rendered at the grassroots level are the steps for strengthening democracy in the country. Effective implementation would ensure the empowerment of the marginalised sections of the Indian society. Indian tribal areas are bestowed with huge mineral wealth. Expanding liberal economy without restricting corporate houses can multiply the problems for the tribal India. In this context, the provisions of the Act relating to empowerment of the Gram Sabha for consultation on land acquisition within its jurisdiction, resettling persons affected by such projects only after consultation with the Gram Sabha or Panchayat at the appropriate level, are indicative of a strong will on part of our policy makers. Despite the comprehensive provisions of empowerment, there are certain gaps in the enactment and implementation that leaves the scope for misinterpretation and violating the spirit of the Act. In place of taking approval from the Gram Sabha or consulting Gram Sabha, the approval is taken from Panchayat at upper tier. The Gram Sabha, the most powerful platform recognised by the Act is strategically avoided (Biswas 2015: 50–54).

Centre Government's Efforts to Make PESA a Great Success

Centre government has taken numerous steps to realise the goals set by the Act. In this field special assistance of Planning Commission, Ministry of Panchayati Raj and the Indian Law Institute has been taken by the Government. Special efforts are being made in the field to protect the rights of the Gram Sabha and Panchayats at the village level. Ministry of Panchayati Raj (MOPR) commissioned the Indian Law Institute for the formulation of the appropriate changes in the state laws concerned, with an objective to assist the state governments in making necessary amendments in existing laws in consultation with their respective Departments of Law.

MOPR has constituted three committees: (i) Under the B.D. Sharma on 'Model Guidelines to vest Gram Sabha with powers envisaged in PESA', (ii) Raghav Chandra sub-committee on 'Land Alienation, Displacement, Rehabilitation and Resettlement' and, (iii) A.K. Sharma sub-committee on 'Minor Forest Produce'. These committees furnished their reports for further action to the ministry. A Committee was constituted under the chairmanship of Dr T. Haque in (2010), to suggest measures on ownership, price fixation, value addition and marketing of minor forest produce. Committee submitted its report in 2011 and on the recommendation, mechanism for Minor Forest Produce through minimum support price, by a centrally sponsored scheme was introduced. A committee on harmonisation of the Central laws with the provisions of the PESA was constituted in December 2011 under the Union Law Secretary. Committee suggested some amendments in the existing central laws. Ministries concerned in the GOI are being requested to expedite the process of amendment in the laws. In 2013, a special scheme was launched in the name of late Prime Minister Rajiv

Gandhi 'Rajiv Gandhi Sashakikaran Abhiyan (RSPSA)' in order to strengthen Gram Sabha in PESA area. It provides for deployment of one mobiliser in each Gram Sabha and one coordinator at block/and district levels.

Himachal Pradesh Panchayati Raj Act

On the lines of the PESA Act, PRIs were also extended to the Scheduled Areas of H.P. in 1997. H.P. Panchayati Raj Second Amendment Act came into force on 15 November 2000 (HP Rural Development and Panchayati Raj Department 2000: 1) with the brief to implement the constitutional provisions of the 73rd Amendment in the Himachal Tribal Area. Various Notifications No. PCH-HA(1) 2006–111, rules in exercise of powers conferred by the sub section (2) of section 186 read with section 97-C, F, G, H, lot HP Panchayati Raj Act, 1994 have been made. These Notifications and PESA Act 1996 gave wide range of powers to the Gram Sabha to manage their affair by adopting the principles of good governance. These are: accountability, effective participation of the masses in decision-making, efficiency, transparency, and social auditing, etc. Role and scope of Gram Sabha as the legislative body of panchayat has also been augmented. At the grassroots level, Gram Sabha is an institution based on the principle of direct democracy. Adult community of the area directly participate in deciding and implementing their development goals. Its viability in the local government system has increased drastically. Under the system local people have been given extensive powers to participate in the governance, execution and accounting process of the development programmes. Gram Sabha has been empowered as the voice of the community, and has been allowed freedom to make decisions related to its own affairs. Gram Sabha as an institution of direct democracy is empowered to social auditing of the Panchayat's functions. Power of social auditing is a step in the field of good governance and in realisation of the dream of real democracy.

In the globalised world, when the tribal societies have also been identified and recognised at the international level by the UNO, it is important to give Constitutional position to the representative bodies to negotiate on the behalf of the community with the outer world which is going to leave an impact on their society. Collective voice of the community is always a strong democratic way to put its interest before the more powerful class. Besides, the legal provisions, environment of any system plays important role in determining the working of the system. Legislative provisions need humane environment in which the tribal societies can realise the importance of the PESA as a strong step to empower them to democratically manage their distinct identity within the purview of the Indian Constitution. Side by side they should be prepared to deconstruct those institutions which do not comply with the universal democratic values along with unhealthy practices based on the man-made inequalities (Hazra 2010: 29–38).

Features of PESA Act

Notwithstanding anything contained under part IX of the Constitution, the legislature of a state shall not make any law under that part which is inconsistent with any of the following features, namely:

1. A state legislation on the Panchayats that may be made shall be in consonance with the customary law, social and religious practices and traditional management practices of community resources;
2. Every Gram Sabha shall be competent to safeguard and preserve the traditions and customs of the people, their cultural identity, community resources and the customary mode of dispute resolution;
3. Gram Sabha or the Panchayat at the appropriate level shall be consulted before making the acquisition of the land in the scheduled areas for the development projects and before resetting or rehabilitating persons affected by such project in the scheduled area, the actual planning and implementation of the projects in the Scheduled Areas shall be coordinated at the state level;
4. Recommendations of the Gram Sabha or the Panchayats at the appropriate level shall be made mandatory prior to grant of prospecting license or mining lease for minor minerals in the scheduled areas;
5. Prior recommendations of the Gram Sabha or the Panchayats at the appropriate level shall be made mandatory for the grant of concession for the exploitation of minor minerals by auction;
6. While endowing Panchayats in the Scheduled areas with such authority as may be necessary to enable them to function as institutions of self-government, a state legislature shall ensure that the panchayats at the appropriate level and the Gram Sabha are endowed specifically with:
   - (i) The ownership of Minor Forest Produces (MFP);
   - (ii) Power to prevent alienation of the land in the schedule areas and to take appropriate action to restore any unlawfully alienated land of a scheduled tribe;
   - (iii) Power to exercise control over money lending to the scheduled tribes;

(iv) Power to exercise control over the institutions and functionaries in all social sector;

(v) Power to control over the local mining plans and resources for such plans including tribal sub plans;

7. The state legislations that may endow panchayats with powers and authority as may be necessary to enable them to function as institutions of self-governance shall contain safeguards to ensure that Panchayats at the higher level do not assume the powers and authority of any Panchayat at the lower level of the Gram Sabha.

8. The state legislature shall make endeavour to follow the pattern of the Sixth Schedule of the Constitution while designing the administrative arrangements in the panchayats at district levels in the scheduled areas (http://www.HimachalPanchayatRajDeptt.) Himachal is among the pioneer states to implement the PESA Act. State government took steps to modify state laws for the compliance of section four of the Act. Ministry of Panchayati Raj (GOI) has confirmed the same. Despite the legal framework during the field study and in course of the periodic agitations by the local people from time to time in three tribal pockets give different picture of the implementation of PESA in the state. There is a general opinion in the area that the manipulative coaxing of the corporate, bureaucrats, local leaders and middleman have defeated the purpose of the PESA. They manage land acquisition, mining lease.

Forest Rights Act (2006) is substantial development in the protection and promotion of the tribal life. Since times immemorial, a large number of people, especially the scheduled tribes have been living in and around forests for a long time in a symbiotic relationship. They have been wholly or partially dependent on forests for their existence. They have also been conserving and using the forests' resources. In modern times with the harsh policies of the Britishers and later post-independence model for development led to the curtailment of centuries old, customary rights of local communities and consolidated the government's role over all forests. This Act was put in place to recognise the claims of the tribals on the forest resources and ownership on land. The Act grants legal recognition to the rights of traditional forest dwelling communities and marks a beginning towards giving communities and the general public, a voice in forest and wildlife conservation. After more than a decade of the enactment of the FRA 2006 effective implementation of the Act has not been taken place. There are certain challenges in the implementation of the FRA. These challenges can be summarised as: (i) deficiency within the Gram Sabha. Institution of Gram Sabha as decision-making body lacks the will and infrastructure and know how to keep their records. (ii) Ambiguity in the formation of Forest Rights Committee. The village is to elect a committee of 10 to 15 members from its residents as a forest rights committee which will process the initial verification of claims and place recommendations before the Gram Sabha. Forest Rights Committee comprising of these people is not effective enough to implement Act in letter and spirit. (iii) Lack of awareness and illiteracy among the native people. (iv) Lack of land record as proof. (v) Lack of inter-departmental coordination. (vi) Harassment by forest officials. Forest Department enjoyed arbitrary powers under the Indian Forest Act 1927. After FRA 2006 these officials are not able to digest the rights given to the tribals. (vii) Attempts to dilute the provisions of the dual Acts PESA and FRA. State governments and the political leadership in different states violate the provisions of the rights of Gram Sabha in the name of ease of doing business and wildlife conservation. It is the order of the day to consider these challenges and the centre and state government should take effective steps in this direction. Implementation of this Act would prove to be panacea against all ills of forest governance and management as well as tribal rights.

Provisions of the PESA Act provide ample scope to the tribal communities for self-governance at the local level. Recognition to their customary laws (within the purview of the constitution) is a step to protect and promote their distinct identity as cultural units also. Right to have control over the local natural resources and their consent for taking any development project within their locality provide them power to maintain and retain their vicinity according to their own wishes. Indian tribes are lagging far behind than the main stream, due to their geographical location and social and economic backwardness. PESA, if implemented in letter and spirit may transform the position of the tribes. Serious question to be addressed is: Will we be able to create an atmosphere by enlightening the tribal community through sincere efforts on the part of the government, civil society and emerging local leadership to bring the last person in the queue to the forefront of the society?

Next part of the chapter is devoted to understand the emerging questions related to the implementation of the PESA Act 1996.

Status of Panchayats in the Schedule V (Tribal)

Whole districts of Kinnaur and Lahaul-Spiti and Development Blocks, namely Pangi and Bharmour of Chamba District comprise the schedule-V area in the state. There are 2 Zila Parishads, namely Kinnaur and Lahual-Spiti and a part of Chamba District of Zila Parishad Chamba, 7 Panchayat Samitis namely Kalpa, Nichar, Pooh, Lahual, Spiti, Bharmour, Pangi and 151 Gram Panchayats constituted in this state in the

Scheduled-V Areas. Following are the number of Gram Panchayats, development block-wise in the Schedule-V Area.

Kinnaur – 65

1. Kalpa : 23
2. Nichar : 18
3. Pooh : 24

Lahual-Spiti – 41

1. Lahual : 28
2. Spiti : 13

Chamba – 45

1. Bharmour : 29
2. Pangi : 16

Effectiveness of PESA

Based on the analysis of ground realities in scheduled areas of Orissa, Jharkhand, Chhattisgarh, Madhya Pradesh and Himachal Pradesh it can be concluded that Gram Sabha do not yet have any kind of ownership of Minor Forest Product (MFP). Awareness level in the Gram Sabha as well as in the Gram Panchayat/other PRIs ownership control and management of MFP and awareness of their extensive rights about the decentralised planning, devolution is very low. On the other hand the state confirmatory Act does not have adequate provision to empower the PRIs in the tribal areas.

The Extension Act has been one of the important legislative measures of recent times which recognised the tribal people's mode of living, their culture and traditions. Unfortunately most of the states have not shown enough zeal and enthusiasm in translating this legislation into practice by making required provisions in their respective Panchayat Acts. The satisfying aspect is that a beginning has been made. There are reservations and hurdles in implementing the Act in its entirety. But it is expected by the centre and state governments to give momentum to the decentralisation. The governments will take effective steps with the growth of human capabilities in the tribal areas. PESA will prove to be effective as constitutional measures to achieve the goals of deepening democracy and good governance (Sharda 2010: 115). Against this optimism the location of the tribals and SC population in the society is not satisfactory after liberalisation and privatisation of professional education. Privatisation of higher education on the socially disadvantaged is significant as it seems social mobility prospects among aspiring SCs and STs ... professional education is not accessible to large sections of SCs and STs as it does not facilitate reservations as mandated in the education, which means that their chances of employment are rather bleak. Due to expensive professional education 'a high proportion of entrants into general higher education. Second there are no reservation in private sector employment where large scale employment opportunities are currently found, SCs and STs are either left out or become educated unemployed (*Yojna*, August 2018: 23–25). The pace of reforms or programme implementation is a function of many factors including bandwidth of the government, challenges posed by the vested interests to thwart reforms and so forth (*Yojna*, June 2018: 13–16).

Himachal is one of the hilly states of India. It attained statehood on 25 January 1971. In the short span it has achieved prominent position in the development index of the country. The state has diverse geography and vegetation. People in the state are innocent and hardworking. It's an agrarian society with rural dominance. It's a trans feudal society. Caste, class and patriarchy determine to the socio-economic and political system to large extent. Politically speaking, upper castes have dominance in the power structures at all the levels. Tribal area has its own importance in the state. In Himachal there are three pockets of the tribal population. Kinnaur and Lahaul-Spiti are exclusive tribal districts. In Chamba Pangi and Bharmour these are two tribal pockets. Many small tribal communities are there. Their occupation, culture and living style varies from each other. Kinnaur has effective tribal pocket. Himachal tribes are better developed than other parts of the country. Most of them earn their livelihood through traditional economic activities.

Conclusion

In the globalised world when the tribal societies have also been identified and recognised at the international level by the UNO. It is important to give Constitutional position to the representative bodies to negotiate on the behalf of the community with the outer world which is going to affect their society. The collective voice of the community is always a strong democratic way to put its interest in front of the mighty. Besides, the legal provisional environment of any system plays an important role in determining the working of that system. Legislative provisions need humane environment in which the tribal societies can realise the importance of the PESA as a strong step to empower them to democratically manage their distinct identity within the purview on the Indian Constitution. Side by side they should be prepared to deconstruct those institutions which do not comply with the universal democratic values along with unhealthy practices based on the man-made inequalities (Hazra 2010: 29–38).

12

Marginalised Sections in PRIs in the Tribal Society

The fact that certain castes and tribes are privileged in comparison to others is well documented. By the same logic, certain other castes and tribes are unprivileged in comparison to their better socially endowed castes and tribes (*Yojna*, August 2018: 23–25).

In the Indian society marginalised sections are called 'Dalits'. Dalits are further divided in the sub-sections: women, lower castes, tribes and children. Dalits are those people who have traditionally been exploited and suppressed by the people who are financially well off (upper caste) and enjoy better status in the society due to the cultural ethos and existing institutional arrangements and processes in the Indian Society. On the basis of the given definition of the Dalits, menfolk, caste and class institution (elite) have enjoyed dominance over the women, lower castes and the economically weaker sections of the society. In the pre-Independence period, power was confined to the landed class that had special status in the society. Their economic status was also associated with their powerful position in the formal and informal institutions of governance. In the princely states, as well as in the British India they were a part of the power system. Common masses were 'the deprived strata' in both the systems.

After independence political equality has been legally rendered to all sections of the society through the Constitution of India; right to vote, right to contest the election, criticise the government are the significant political rights of the Indian citizens. Constitutional equality (Article 14–18) was given to the Indians irrespective of the manmade differences.

Indian society experienced deep rooted gender, caste and class based inequalities. The system needs conscious efforts to realise the democratic values aspired for the Indian society by our constitution makers. Since independence, incumbent governments have taken various legislatives steps, policy decisions, and planned efforts to bring the deprived sections on the pedestal of equality. In spite of all the steps in the last seventy years the process of transformation is slow. Power centres, formal and informal, depict the level of inequality and the status of the marginalised in the society. Social profile of the parliamentarians and the legislators since 1952 indicates that majority of them belong to the elite section of society. Most of them are either the scions of the royal families, rest of them belong to the elite section of society. Common people have less chance in the power race at the different levels. Lower sections from the rural background have had fairly little representation in the Parliament and state legislatures.

It is only after the 73rd Amendment through reservation that doors have been opened to the Dalits. Analytically, it has been observed that among the Dalits also, a section having better economic position constitute the elite of that section. Among the Dalits also, the better off enjoy the status of the elite. Vertically in India the 'upper castes' have better position in the villages. Rural society is based on a rigid caste system. In the tribal areas also they have a rigid stratification system. One particular section of the society enjoys better status as compared to the rest. Tribal societies which are more close to the Hindu culture and have adopted the Hindu practices, follow the Hindu caste system. Others practise the system as it suits them. Lower caste psyche, to appease this class, is more prevalent in the areas where 'Jajmani' system is in practice. In comparison to the political change, social change is relatively slow in the Indian society. India has successfully adapted to political democracy, and political institutions have been working efficiently for the last seventy years. Periodic elections, constitutional measures to change the governments, the role of judiciary as the protector and defender of democracy are conspicuous examples of political democracy in the country. Traditional institutions like caste, class and patriarchy have dominant role in weaving the social, economic and political fabric of the society. To enquire about this fact an empirical study was undertaken in the tribal areas of the Himachal Pradesh.

Community Opinion About Dalit Participation in the Tribal Areas

By better location of the lower castes in the rural power system, social change would also be accomplished. Empowered lower castes would serve as a catalyst to reduce inequalities in the Indian society. Rural India which also includes the tribal society of India that comprises 8.6 per cent of the total population has distinct social systems. Tribals are already on the margins due to their geographical, demographic conditions. After seventy years of Independence they are still on the margins. This section, the poorest among the poor, is struggling to meet their basic needs of life. They do not get basic medical facilities, sufficient calories and education for their children. In such conditions, their effective participation in the power system is rather distant possibility. It is necessary to understand their plight.

In Himachal Pradesh all the tribal communities have their stratification system. Caste and class are dominating variables. In the Lahaul and Pangwal societies, Hindu caste patterns are followed. In Kinnaur, occupation and economic status have a distinct role in the stratification of society. Kinnaur society is highly stratified. Caste and class, both the institutions, have close relationship with the power institutions. Unlike most of the tribes Kinnauras have typical caste ridden society. According to the Census 1901, 'Rajput society in the hill states are usually agriculturists and some are employed in the state, subdued the weak one and used to annex the territory and services'. These people were known as Khoshiyas in Kinnaur. They are the descendants of Khasas. Khasas organised themselves into families and villages, elected Mavi or Mavana, meaning strongest person among themselves. The strongest Mavana subdued the weaker one and used to annex his territory. Thus, in this process whole region was split into small units called Mavanas (Chauhan 1998: 111). The menial and lower castes are known as Kolis. The Kolis are supposed to have sprung from the Kanets through the practice of one brother in the family being told to perform necessary but degrading services, such as the disposal of carcasses of dead cattle. In the same way the various craftsmen are believed to be Kanets in origin, which have become distinguished by their peculiar operations. They are called Chomang and Domang. The former includes shoemakers, weavers and the like, the latter blacksmiths and carpenters (Gazetteer of The Shimla Hill States 1910: 22; Chauhan 1998). Their political history explains the caste character of the Kinnaura polity. In twelfth century AD Kinnauras had Char-bhai system. In this system Mukhiya (headman) and Char (revenue collector and in-charge of criminal matters) both were from the Khoshiya community. Khoshiyas in the tribal community are Rajputs. Rajputs are either known for their warrior skills or as the landlords or persons of exceptional skills. Caste like Brahmin has no reference in the system. Rajputs enjoyed better status in the political life of the society. Other two places in the Char-bhai system were marked as the lower caste. Halamandi and Toknya (guards of the village) were from Chomang community. Chomang community is the service provider of the society. After the Char-bhai system with the introduction of the 'Thakurai' in Kinnaur, the institution of Char-bhai was replaced by the 'charas' (single person who was responsible for the village administration). Charas was the link between the Thakur (a person who had control over the Prangna) and village people. In the village governance Rajput community always enjoyed better status. When the people of Kinnaur were asked about the Dalits' role in politics after the introduction of PRI system under PESA, 50 per cent community respondents replied that the Dalits have involvement in the PRIs working. During the different visits in the tribal areas and interaction with the tribal students it was observed that caste system is very strong in the Kinnaura tribe. Broadly there are two castes: upper and the lower. Both the castes follow strictly customary practices. They do not share food with each other. The lower caste people restrict themselves in entering the higher caste people's houses. The younger generation also follows the same practices in their native places. Reservation has provided them some space in the caste ridden society.

To bring equality in a society where inequality is deep rooted, special efforts need to be made. In the developed countries it is called 'affirmative' action. In India, it is named as reservation. Dalit section of the society remained suppressed for the centuries together. During the national movement, leaders like Gandhi, Ambedkar and JP supported the idea of social, economic reforms to bring equality in the society. Gandhi championed the cause of gender equality. In order to facilitate these objectives, special provisions were made in the Constitution for a proportional representation of SCs/STs in the Parliament, state legislatures and services. But the reservation benefits were denied to women. The extremely marginalised sections failed to get the benefits despite reservation. Benefit of reservation also benefited the creamy layer of the lower castes. The deprived position is more or less stagnant. Position of the employment in the private sector also indicates that women and the lower strata of the society is still on the back foot of the society. In the formal political institutions in the Parliament and state legislatures SCs and STs had their quota before 1993. Women had little chances to be part of the decision-making process. From that perspective reservation through 73rd Amendment ushered into the area of the placement of poor section of the society in the power echelons. Regarding the reservation community respondents 54 per cent favoured reservation, 22 per cent respondents had negative view and 24 per cent had no opinion. Although higher caste people crib on the reservation issue but they still say yes to the reservation on the economic basis.

According to the system approach there is close relationship between system and its environment. Political system works in the ecology (social, economic and cultural system). Each system affects the other and vis-à-vis the other systems. In all the societies' role of the formal governmental institutions is shaped and limited by the informal groups, political attitudes and multitude of interpersonal relationships (Almond and Powell 1966: 17). Indian political system works in the social and economic system that is dominated by the feudal ethos. Still the upper castes and economic well-off people have their influence in the formal and informal institutions' decision-making process. Reservation has created space for the deprived sections of the society, but their effective participation is a big question. After the two decades of the New Panchayati Raj (NPR) implementation in case of the Uttar Pradesh Panchayati Raj Election 2015 media exposed the women's plight and their level of awareness. Although they were candidates for the PRIs election but they were not aware about the name of the Chief Minister of their state. Empowerment does not stand for the numerical strength unless they are able to take effective decisions.

Community members were asked about the position of the traditional institutions and procedures in the decision-making process of the PRIs. Almost in all the areas of the state, the response was similar. Overall 38 per cent asserted that the elite have special status in the decision-making and 34 per cent viewed it the other way round, while 28 per cent refused to share their opinion.

For centuries together in India, Varna system was replaced by the caste system. In the caste system two basic features emerged: social rigidity and lower castes, they were deprived from doing certain functions in the society. These social practices affected the political and economic field. In the political institutions these sections were considered secondary citizens. Gradually they became deprived sections of the society, and they accepted this status before and after the independence in general. After four decades of the Independence due to the collective efforts of the government, non-governmental organisations, leaders from the deprived sections as well as the leaders who championed the cause of social justice, the marginalised people got special status in the form of reservation in the PRIs. Empirically it is found that there is difference between state backed participation and people's participation on their own initiative. Community respondents were asked about the effectiveness of the deprived sections in the Gram Sabha and the PRIs.

As many as 39 per cent of the respondents agreed with the view that they are not heard and do not have effective position in the decision-making process. Another 37 per cent disagreed with this opinion. Further, they were asked about variables that are the factors for the discrimination. Twenty-nine per cent of the respondents believed that social status is an important factor which prevents them from raising questions, 13 per cent of the respondents believed that economic status is an important factor, 14 per cent believe that sexual status is an important factor, 16 per cent believe that educational status is an important factor and 28 per cent of the respondents believe that none of the given status factors prevents them from raising the questions.

Majority of the respondents believed that social status is an important factor which prevents them from raising the questions but side by side they also believed that economic, sexual and educational status are the important factors responsible for their restricted role. Multiple variables have their role in determining the participation in formal rural power system. To understand the opinion of the community respondents, they were asked about their response on the issue of dominance of elite in the PRIs and processes. Nearly 48 per cent agreed with the view that the persisting institutions (caste, class) and male chauvinism persist in the society. The higher caste, class and male dominance is still prevailing in the system. Traditional institutions have strong grip over the socio-political system to overcome these impediments. Respondents view was 27 per cent of the respondents believed that to some extent women and SC participation can be increased by literacy and economic independence, 56 per cent of the respondents believed that to a great extent women and SC participation can be increased by literacy and economic independence and 17 per cent of the respondents believed that women and SC participation can never be increased by literacy and economic independence. In their opinion social inequalities and social taboos could not be checked by economic equality and educational status easily. Majority of there were in favour of investing on the human capital to make the system effective.

Kinnaura tribes are progressive and they are optimistic about future development. Their attitude towards women literacy, especially among SCs, and economic independence of the marginalised sections, is important from the angle of the effectiveness of the involvement of the marginalised sections in the working of the PRIs. They also confessed that women and SCs face social problems which reduce their efficiency to perform their role being leaders. Reservation in the local bodies has provided space to the marginalised sections in the political institutions. With the corporate intervention in the tribal areas social paradigms have also changed. Tribal economy had two main heads: family income and common property resources. Landless section and women both enjoyed better position due to common property resources. With the acquisition of the forest lands by government and corporate houses these two sections were marginalised socially and economically. Forty-three per cent of the respondents believed that women or lower castes face social problems when they take part in the PRI elections, 21 per cent faced political problems, 12 per cent of them faced economic problems, only 5 per cent faced administrative problems and 19 per cent of the respondents believed that as women or lower caste (SC) they face no problem at any level when they take part in the PRI elections and working. Kinnaura tribe has strong traditional political system. Caste, class and gender hegemony is dominating in the political field. Lower caste people and women participate in the informal processes.

Poverty from the perspective of Human Development is a 'denial of choices and opportunities for living a tolerable life' (UNDP 1997). Poverty is a multi-dimensional phenomenon that includes liquid money, material and determinants like nutrition and proper living conditions. Marginalised sections are those which are deprived of tolerable conditions. Twenty-nine per cent of the respondents think that marginalised people show their presence by political participation in social and civil movements at the grassroots level, 24 per cent feel that margnialised people show their regular presence at the grassroots level, 14 per cent think that the marginalised people raise questions at the grassroots level and 33 per cent of the respondents think that political participation of the marginalised people have always contributed in the working of Panchayats, as well as at the Gram Sabha level. Formal power structures are dominated by the traditional institutions whereas the marginalised sections make efforts to register their presence wherever they get the opportunity to do so.

Religious Practices and the Tribal Power Structures

Institution of 'deity' known as Devta or Devi is very common among the tribals of Himachal. They perform every activity in all the spheres with the customary permission of the Devta or Devi. The institution of the untouchability is prevalent in the society due to their association with purity and impurity of these functions. Devi and Devta prohibit people belonging to certain castes from performing certain functions. It is observed that Devi and Devta are indispensable functionaries of the system.

Religious institutions and practices have an explicit relationship with local political system. Respondents were asked about the role of local 'devta'. Nineteen per cent of the respondents think that local deity system promotes their chance of political participation at the village level, 33 per cent think that local deity system hampers their chances of political participation at village level and 48 per cent of the respondents refrained from expressing their opinion about the local deity system promoting or hampering their chances of political participation at village level. Tribal society is regulated by the institution of local deity and customary laws.

Customary methods of dispute settlement are very common among the tribals. Forty-six per cent of the respondents believed in customary methods of dispute settlement. Thirty-five per cent responded in negative. There were 19 per cent of the respondents who kept mum on this issue. Majority of the respondents believed in the customary methods of dispute settlement in all three blocks of the district. It is evident that customary practices are common among the tribes. At village level, most of the times, cases are settled by their traditional institutions. Community decisions have to be obeyed by the people. Disregard of these decisions sometimes leads to the excommunication of the offender.

Political-Economic Dimensions of Tribes in the Early Twenty-First Century

RTI Act 2005 is a progressive right. It provides an opportunity to the masses to exercise their democratic rights towards making the system more transparent and accountable. It is a channel which would minimise the flaws of the bureaucratic state also. Data regarding the awareness of masses about RTI is encouraging. Forty-seven per cent of the respondents were aware about RTI which is an important tool to protect and promote the rights of masses for getting the desired information, 21 per cent were not aware about the RTI Act and 32 per cent of the respondents were silent about this.

Respondents graph indicates tribal people are aware about the RTI Act. This Act is an important step in the promotion of transparency and accountability at the lowest level. This is one of the most important developments of the Indian System. It can prove to be a decisive step in the field of sound political and administrative system in the country. When the respondents were asked about the application of the right, it was observed that 19 per cent respondents had asked for information under the RTI only once, 11 per cent of the respondents had used RTI twice, three per cent of the respondents had used RTI for more than two times and 65 per cent of the respondents had never used RTI. Majority of the respondents have not used RTI and only five per cent of the respondents have used RTI for more than two times. There is a gap between the awareness and utilisation of the RTI Act. Majority of masses have never sought information.

Tribals, from the beginning, have banked on forests. Forests have always been their lifeline. Their livelihood, their health, their professional life as well as their identity is associated with the forests. To specify their identity, cultural practices and source of income, Minor Forest Act 2006 was enacted. It is a step to protect their forest rights. Thirty-six per cent of the respondents are aware of the Forest Right Act 2006, 42 per cent of the respondents do not have the knowledge about the Forest Right Act 2006 and 22 per cent of the respondents have not expressed their opinion on either side.

Majority of the respondents are not aware of the Forest Rights Act 2006. Forest Rights Act, 2006 is a landmark step to protect the Forest Rights of the Tribes. Jungles have always been the natural source of livelihood for the tribes. The British, through the promulgation of various acts (1927 Forest Act) affected the interests of the natives negatively. After more than five decades of Independence, Minor Forest Act was enacted. The Act empowers the tribes to assert their forests rights. It provides space to the tribal folk to preserve their tribal life without outside interventions. But masses are not aware about these rights (RTI and FRA). People who are aware about these rights complained that forest department has a complicated system and forest officials do not permit them to use these rights. Those who were aware of MFP 42 per cent are not using their right on Minor Forest Produce (MFP), 37 per cent of the respondents are not aware and not using their rights related to MFP and 21 per cent of the respondents have not expressed their opinion on either side.

All over the country with the opening of the avenues for the corporates in the far flung areas, the most affected section is the tribe. Big business houses have intervened in most of the tribal belts of the country to get an access to the mineral and other natural resources. Their interventions have adversely affected the tribal world. Seventy-six per cent of the respondents think that the development process under the corporate houses has a negative impact on nature, 11 per cent of the respondents do not think so and 13 per cent of the respondents have not expressed their opinion on either side.

Majority of the respondents think that development process under corporates has a negative impact on nature. At large, New Economic Policy (NEP) 1991 resulted in Globalisation-Privatisation. Free economic activities, growth of corporate houses and their intervention in the remotest areas affected the tribals enormously. Orissa, Bihar, Madhya Pradesh and most of the states having tribal societies have been affected by the NEP. In Kinnaur maximum hydro power projects have either been installed or proposed. Home stay is another government sponsored scheme to strengthen the tourism in the state. As some of the questions reflect, people have strong inclination towards their traditions.

People in Kinnaur are not happy with the corporate activities in the system. They strongly oppose the corporate activities and hold them responsible for the disintegration of tribal system. Only 19 per cent of the respondents believe that installation of hydroelectric projects in their area is good, 62 per cent of respondents perceive installation of hydro-electric projects in their areas are not favourable to the tribal system. Ten per cent respondents have not expressed their opinion on either side.

Conclusions

Present status of the tribal societies indicates that the tribal societies are in the stage of transition. Societies are not comfortably adopting the social changes. Their traditional institutions and roles are accepted reality of the tribal society. Social reality does not mean that the stagnation is a feature of the tribal living. Political adaptation, educational graph of the tribes and their persistent adaptation to the medical services are the indicators of fusion of modern tradition. All these developments, their slow and steady awareness about legislative constitutional developments indicate the development of the tribes. It has been experienced by the studies conducted in the Himachal tribal area.

13

Tribal Communities in the Era of Liberalisation, Privatisation and Globalisation (LPG)

Case Study of Himachal Tribes

According to the preamble of the Indian Constitution every individual will be equal before the law and will get equal opportunities and social justice in the future India. To realise these ideals, provisions have been laid down in the Constitution in the form of fundamental rights (Article 15, 16, 20–30) and Directive Principles of the state policy (Article 36–51). In case of the vulnerable sections of the society (Scheduled-castes, Scheduled-tribes, Minorities, and Women) these objectives and rights are of immense importance. Tribal people living in the remote parts of the country due to the tough terrain, ignorance for the centuries remained secluded and could not get the benefits of the modernity and scientific innovations at large. In case of India lopsided development-strategies and non-involvement of the masses in governance and developmental activities after independence led to the slow pace of development. Nehru, Elwin, and Gandhi; all the three had the common view that utilisation of tribal manpower in production was the only decisive method of their development. Nehru was in favour of using modern technology for maximisation of production in both the industrial and agriculture sector. He did not accept the Gandhian idea of village self-sufficiency and decentralisation. Nehru wanted that the state should control all means of production but Gandhi wanted property should lie in the hands of village community. Elwin empirically realised the tribal situation and supported Gandhi's stand, and emphasised tribal rights to forest land as well as the use of their primitive technology in production (for details see Chandra Rath 2006: 65–91). Nehru's approach was adopted after Independence to deal with the tribal society of India. Local initiatives were not encouraged to manage their social, economic and political issues. Indigenous practices were not considered which they followed for times immemorial, and a new system was implemented without taking the local masses into confidence. All these developments led to a gap between perception and practice. During the first fifty years after independence, the planning process in India has failed to narrow the disparities between the tribal and non-tribal populations, which according to Andre Gunder Frank (1969) has rather accentuated the dominant relationships and reinforced unequal relationships between super and subordinate groups (Rath 2006: 17). Marginalised communities, including tribals have failed to derive benefits from the developmental programmes.

Centralised planning, ineffective or to large extent non-working local government, one dominant party system in the country took its toll. Political democracy meant for the people was 'to elect the national and state governments'. Economic democracy stood for dependence on the state for the economic avenues and needs. Less importance was given to the development of micro economic avenues based on indigenous practices. Social democracy was merely constitutional equality. Traditional institutions, practices based on feudal system dominated the social system. Gender, caste, and class based inequalities have been all pervasive in the Indian society. State failed to assess the needs and ambition of the masses. Neither were the masses able to get opportunity to decide their needs nor were there channels to fulfil those socio economic and political needs till the Seventy Third Amendment Act was enacted in 1993. This Amendment is an initial step to provide opportunities to the rural masses to locate themselves in the Indian democratic system which includes socio-economic and political dimensions. In 1990s there were two developments in the system that had direct impact on the Indian masses. Seventy Third Amendment and the New Economic Policy (NEP). NEP provided opportunities to the corporate world to enter the tribal areas of the country which are rich in natural resources. PESA 1996 on the lines of Seventy Third Amendment empowered the tribal communities legally; to protect and promote their interests in the changing world. Under the Act, multiple steps have been taken by the government to mould the existing system to enhance the capability and capacity of the tribal community to decide its fortune. The ideal form of tribal development, is therefore, more appropriately identified as non-industrial but pro-local, one which intends to make local resources and environment more congenial to providing for a stable livelihood for the tribes (Rath 2006: 21). Steps under PESA are important in the present context when the process of liberalisation, privatisation, and globalisation has opened the doors of the tribal world to the corporate activities. The contractors and business community, who have links with politicians funding them at regular intervals (in the elections and for other personal purposes), have gained unlimited rights to plunder the supposedly protected forest wealth and resort to illegal mining. Tribal areas are rich in natural resources. New Economic Policy aimed to liberalise the economy for the competing entrepreneurs within the country or outside the country has provided a convenient way to the corporate sector to enter the tribal areas for corporate activities. These developments have considerable impact on the tribal communities. In most of the cases tribal areas are unexplored and rich storehouse of natural resources. These resources have potential input for the modern market driven system. It has been realised by the corporate world. In the last two decades in the remote areas where the tribals have their habitats has been exposed to the external interventions under the NEP. In the tribal areas corporate houses established the industrial units/installed hydro power projects or unscientific mining has become common feature of the area. Innocent vulnerable section (tribals) of the Indian society is not able to understand the intricacies and complexities of the development process which pose a challenge to their physical and cultural identity.

Vulnerable sections such as: Scheduled Caste, Scheduled Tribes, minorities, and women, of the Indian society are still far behind the rest of the population in spite of the elaborate provisions and legislative measures to improve their condition. One of the most vulnerable sections among them is the tribes. According to Census 2011 report, the population of Scheduled Tribes in the country is approximately 100 million, consisting about 8.4 per cent of the total population. As per census report literacy rate among tribals is 47 per cent and it is far below the country overall. The female literacy rate among tribals is far lower as compared to the female literacy rate in the country. Their economic condition also indicates their overall plight. Majority of tribals constitute labour work force, though their participation in work is declining, but not steadily. Workers among tribals can be divided into three categories – main workers (43.10%), marginal workers (7.61%) and non-workers (49.29%). More than half of the rural tribal population is found to be below the poverty line as per the survey available with Ministry of Rural Development GOI. According to the Human Development Index (HDI) at the national level tribals are far behind the mainstream population in terms of literacy, employment and mortality rate. The school attendance rate (5–14 age group) among the tribes is quite low. The tribes have second largest share of landless people after SC population. Although the tribals are less chronically unemployed persons rather than non-tribals in rural and urban areas, but their Monthly Per Capita Expenditure (MPCE) is lower than the SC population. Tribal people live in the remote parts of the country. Due to tough terrain, ignorance and lopsided development strategies tribes have failed to get the benefits of the developmental programmes. This is evident from the Human Development Index. Keeping in mind these developments, a primary study has been conducted to evaluate the impact of the policy programmes in the last two decades on the tribal community at large. Study area are the tribal areas of the Himachal Pradesh. Five rivers are the main source of the hydro power in the state. Many mega hydro power projects have been installed in this area. Corporate world explored the tribal region to exploit the water resources in this area. Participatory observation, informal discussions with the local people and community leaders is the major source of information. Some leaders, NGOs were also consulted on these issues through mobile phone. The questions addressed in this study have been designed to ascertain the extent of impact of the state policy based on principles of liberalisation, privatisation, and globalisation on the tribal community. Is this policy compatible with the socialistic (social-economic-equality and justice) and liberal (political, economic freedom along with protection and promotion of their own culture) ideals of the Indian Constitution. NEP gave space to the entrepreneurs from within the country and outside the country. Policy of liberalisation and privatisation has its ramification on the Indian tribes also. The questions addressed in this chapter are how far the state policy based on the principles of liberalisation, privatisation, and globalisation affected the tribal people. Water pollution, air pollution is also affecting the health of the people. Cancer patients, tuberculosis and pulmonary diseases are increasing day by day.

Himachal has five big rivers of the north: Beas, Ravi, Satluj, Chenab and Yamuna. It has immense scope for hydel power (20,463 MW). Most of the hydro power projects in the state are situated in the tribal areas. Some of them are mega projects. Total Power generation is 6,606 mw at present. These projects have affected the physical and human environment in these areas. Widening of roads with the use of explosives has led to landslides, air pollution and devastation of the bio-diversity in the tribal area. In Kinnaur Satluj basin of Kinnaur district, which accounts for 9,728.25 MW hydro power potential, Baspa, Karcham-Wangtoo, Keshang, Sanjay Viduyut Pariyojna, Shanan projects have already been commissioned. Construction of tunnels is one of the main causes of drying up of several springs and Satluj River. Satluj is the lifeline of the Kinnaura people. It has become a dumping site for the power projects that causes deterioration in the quality of water. Bio-diversity has also been affected in the area and their traditional economy based on the forest resources have also been mitigated by the construction of power projects. Uprooting of jungles has reduced the Chilgoza (one of the variety of dry fruits) production which was a prominent source of their livelihood. Kinnaur is famous for quality apples; people attribute the decrease in crop production to the activities of these power projects. Climate change is also caused by the on-going construction. Decreasing snow fall, unpredictable weather has disturbed their horticulture patterns. Nehru and Elwin believed that tribal poverty was created by outsiders and not evolved from within. After Independence, the new generations of outsiders like the refugees and government employees colluded with the old generation, leading to poverty among tribes. After the NEP third generation of corporates have been playing the negative role of exploiting the tribals for their own benefits.

In the tribal area demographic patterns and occupations are co-related. Land owning class, mostly belonging to higher castes, orchardists are educated, and enjoy social and political power. Other class is either landless or marginal farmers (belonging to the traditional service provider class, economically weak, considered to be untouchables, less educated, and after reservation they have merely a physical presence in the local institutions manoeuvered by the land owning class). Demographic patterns have their impact on the political and social life in the area. The former is mainly the orchardist class having little dependence on forests. They have been benefitted by the corporate interventions in the area. The latter are traditional service providers, less educated, having small pieces of land. They are less exposed to the outer world. It is not easy for them to compete with outsiders for jobs in the open market, nor do they have permanent assets like land, and means for ensuring a decent subsistence. Forests are the main source of their livelihood. This class is facing challenges from the corporate world. Tribal people are not able to protect and promote their age-old culture. A study by B.R. Thakur in (2012) also concluded that transformation has occurred in the tribal areas of HP. Literacy rate, their style of living and crop patterns have also changed. Traditional institutions and their roles have also changed. Besides, the change in cultural milieu (in the last two decades) is also taking place in the economic activities. People have abandoned their traditional professions like pastoral activities in the upper Kinnaur and agro economy in the lower Kinnaur. In all the areas 'shamlat land' of the village is acquired for the projects. Traditionally, the marginalised farmers who reared livestock with the support of the common village land are not able to do so now. They have been affected by the growing capital based economic activities in the tribal area. Overall in all the areas livestock figures have gone down in the last two decades. Gaddis were known for their livestock, but due to corporate activities in Chamba they are also not keen to continue this profession.

Himachal is known for its beauty. Tribal areas possess virgin beauty. There is immense scope for tourism in both Kinnaur and Lahaul. People from within the country or outside India love to visit the tribal Himachal. Government of Himachal Pradesh has initiated schemes like Home Stay in the tribal areas. Entrepreneurs from the plains also take land on lease for adventure tours. Natives of the area either run home stay or the poor natives perform petty jobs during the tourist season. Landless people of the area are not getting much benefit from these schemes. Home stays are also run by those who hold prime properties in the area. This scheme has benefited some households in the Kinnaur. But they are not happy with this type of tourist activity in the tribal area. Local people are of the opinion that foreigners have different lifestyle which is affecting the youth of the area. They copy the foreigners in Lahaul, and in some of the parts of Kullu young generation is addicted to opium because of the constant presence of foreigners who come here for such activities. It is harmful to the society and the culture also. Kinnauras feel that they are not able to get the benefits of the adventure tourism due to their ignorance and lack of experience in this field. Outsiders are able to manage better tourism avenues in the tribal areas. They are able to convince the private landowners and they manage to get land of the locals on lease for tourism purpose. Job scenario for the locals in tourism sector is bleak. Local youth lack communication skills. They are not formally trained in hospitality. They lack vocational training. Kinnauras are employed here to perform petty jobs and they get minimum wages. Generally they quit their jobs in the power projects also due to the terms and conditions of the employers. When one social activist in the area was asked about the employment opportunities for the locals he strongly asserted that these companies are not interested in engaging the locals. They create such situations that force the locals to quit. It is also evident from the rising number of floating population in the area that is roughly 30 per cent of the total population of Kinnaur. Labour force comprises of people from Nepal, Bihar and Bengal. In the Rarang village of Kinnaur migrants have their separate colony. Local people during the visit complained that the migrant labour disturb their system. They use forest wood for fuel and cut trees in the forests which is against their culture. Migrant labour has also affected the traditional professionals (Oarse and Domangs) in the area. In the construction works local people deploy Biharis and Rajasthanis due to their expertise in construction and wood work. People in the tribal area have developed a taste for modern construction models, commonly found in cities. Most of the houses in the tribal areas these days are RCC structures. They are not compatible with the climatic conditions of the tribal area, yet people in the far flung areas have concrete buildings which were not common in the tribal areas before 1990. Local masons, labour and carpenters are not able to compete with the experts from Bihar and Rajasthan. All these developments have affected the job avenues for the local professionals who are unable to get employment after the change in the lifestyle of the tribals.

Paradigms of village society are also changing with the intrusion of corporates in the tribal community. Land owning class of the society has reaped more benefits in the form of compensation for their lands, while poor marginal farmers have failed to get similar benefits in the form of compensation. They had to dispense with their small tracts of land in the land acquisition process, but in lieu of that they either got petty jobs or became unemployed. Ramification of this process is raising disparities in the tribes that is causing factionalism in the society.

Health hazards are rising these days with the change in the life style and pollution in these areas. Water pollution, air pollution is also affecting the health of the people. Number of cancer patients is on the rise. Tuberculosis and pulmonary diseases are increasing day by day in the tribal areas. More cases of hypertension and stress are being reported in the area. It is also confirmed from the local health centre and one of the most eminent physicians of the area (Dr P.C. Negi). Environment is one of the most important issues in the present times when the excessive exploitation of natural resources has created challenges for the nature. Landslides, soil erosion, change in the climatic conditions are important dysfunctional aspects of LPG in tribal areas. Forest dwellers have been displaced from their original places. Little attention is being paid towards their rehabilitation. Legislative measures such as PESA 1996, Forest Rights Act 2006 have been enacted. Implementation of these acts is very poor. Political will to empower the excluded sections (marginalised) of the society is lacking. Sporadic movements by Him Lok Jagriti Manch and Zila Van Adhikar Samiti have been initiated to implement the Forest Rights Act 2006 and PESA Act 1996 effectively. The tribal agitation led by the non-official members of the District Level Committee on 30 December 2018 for the implementation of FRA 2006 and PESA 1996 averred 'bureaucratic ignorance on the provisions of the Forest Rights Act as well as their attitude towards the common people of state ... thousands of claims are hanging fire in district Kinnaur alone at various stages because of lack of bureaucratic action' (reported by *Times Now*).

Regarding the Social Impact Assessment (SIA), and Environment Impact Investment (EIA) committees and their effectiveness, people from different sections from the area were interviewed. NGOs Zila Sangharsh Samiti Kinnaur HP and Him Lok Jagriti Manch both are making efforts to make the people aware regarding the negative impact of power projects on the tribal society. When Ranjit Singh Negi (retired IAS from Maharashtra cadre) was asked about the SIA and EIA he strongly opposed the mega projects and opined that the policy of liberalisation has changed the tribal culture. Tribal people have been exposed to the vices like criminalisation. Many research studies reveal that degradation of tribal life, alienation of tribals are caused by alcohol and money lenders. As is always in the case, the contractors and business community, who have links with politicians funding them at regular intervals have gained unlimited rights to plunder supposedly protected forests wealth and resort to illegal mining. Added to this is the clause of 'public purpose' for which the law sanctions land acquisition but which is done in favour of people, as has been in the case in various parts of the country affecting specially the tribals.

Regarding the job opportunities in both the sectors for Kinnauras, scope is not satisfactory. Mostly the youth in the area is lacking vocational education. Kinnauras employed here perform petty jobs and they get minimum wages. Generally they quit the jobs due to the terms and conditions of the employers. When one social activist was asked about the employment opportunities for the locals he strongly asserted that these companies are not interested in engaging the locals. They create such situations that the locals are forced to leave the job. It is also evident from the rising number of floating population in the area that is roughly 30 per cent of the total population of the state, comprising mainly of Nepali, Bihari and Bengali labour. Migrant labour has also affected the traditional professional workers (Oarse and Domangs) in the area. Problems of resettlement of the tribes are common in all the areas like the central region where industrialisation process started immediately after the first five year plan. Rath (2006) identified those problems 'the present generation of displaced families has no hope of getting a job in the plant; it is not easy for them to compete with outsiders for jobs in the open market, nor do they have assets like land or artisan's means of production for ensuring subsistence. Quality of education among them has not yet reached the expected level; despite having a sound educational infrastructure around them' (63–92). Among the construction workers more and more outsiders are deployed by the locals. Local professionals are not able to get employment. Data given by the JP Corporation indicates discrepancies. When the officials were asked about the employee data they provided information at the time of beginning of the project and did not show the updated data because many local employees had left the job. This also indicates that the NEP is not able to generate employment opportunities for the natives. Paradigms of village society are also changing with the intrusion of corporate culture in tribal community. Landowning class of the society has gained more benefits in form of compensation for their lands while poor marginal farmers have failed to get similar benefits. They had to lose their small landholdings, and in turn either got petty jobs or were rendered jobless. Rising disparity among the tribes is a major fallout of this process that is causing factionalism in the society. In India 'implementation of development projects has been found wanting in planning and policy regulation'. 'Only a minority fraction ... has been relocated (and planned for) by the projects that displaced them,' with the majority having to fend for themselves, and being 'left even poorer than they were before' (Padovani 2016: xiv).

Panchayats Extension to the Scheduled Areas (PESA Act, 1996) is one land mark step in the sphere of tribal empowerment. Through various notifications and amendments in HP Panchayati Raj Act, Gram Sabha and three tiers of PRIs have been given wide ranging powers in the tribal areas. According to PESA 'Every Gram Sabha shall be competent to safeguard and preserve the traditions and customs of the people, their cultural identity, community resources and customary mode of dispute resolution; every Gram Sabha shall: approve the plans, programmes and projects for social and economic development before such plans, programmes and projects are taken for implementation,' (HP PESA Act 1996 {e,f}). It has been observed empirically that implementation of PESA Act is poor in the tribal areas of HP. Rising resentment among the masses and NGOs (Him Sangharsh Samiti, Kinnaur Bachao Andolan and the organisation to implement the FRA), their efforts to protect the tribal society and their rights indicate discontent among the masses of the Scheduled area. In case of hydro power projects, Gram Sabhas complain of not being consulted. Non-official members of the District Level Committee on FRA, along with the people of the Lippa village in Kinnaur organised a protest in Shimla on 30 December 2018. According to the provisions of the Act, land cannot be acquired by government or corporate sector without the permission of the Gram Sabha. But in case of Wangtoo Karcham project, three out of four villages were not consulted. Later on these villages protested against the decision and boycotted the Panchayat elections 2010. In Chamba and Lahaul also people boycotted 2015 Panchayat elections in protest against the hydro power projects. Gram sabhas have been given property rights related to the MFP and other natural resources under FRA 2000, but ignorance among the tribal people is one of the reasons that they are not able to take benefits given to them. Corporate sector is exploiting the natural resources in the tribal areas which genuinely belong to the tribes.

Inferences of the Study

State policies of liberalisation, privatisation, and globalisation have exposed the tribal communities to the corporate sector. The contractors and business community have links with politicians. Business houses appease them with several benefits individually, and provide generous funds to their parties at regular intervals. In lieu of the financial benefits they get unlimited rights to plunder the supposedly protected forest wealth and resort to illegal mining. Added to this is the clause of public purpose 'for which the law sanctions land acquisition, but is manipulated in favour of the corporate houses'; this is a common malady in various parts of the country, affecting the tribals.

Shift in the policy framework in 1991 was not well planned and policies governing corporate houses in the tribal areas were implemented without preparation. Even today tribal people are not aware of the legislative measures, and their right to check the corrupt practices which are not compatible with their system. During the field study in intervals in tribal areas in the years 2012, 2015 and 2017 people admitted that they were not aware of the developments related to the tribal community of the country. Awareness levels have gradually gone up. In the last two decades, no comprehensive policy framework has been worked out in tribal India that would enable them to face challenges from the corporate world in the form of skill development and drive for mass awareness with respect to the developments related to the corporate sector and empowerment of the tribals. Skilled human capital is the need of the day. Tribals are less technically skilled. Tribal enrollment in engineering and other vocational courses is not very impressive at the national as well as at the state level. Human capital and infrastructure in the tribal areas is not sufficient to meet the challenges of the Liberalisation, Privatisation and Globalisation (LPG). Existing system cannot be reformed through a piecemeal approach.

Lopsided development has a negative bearing on the social and cultural milieu of the tribal society. Crime rate is increasing in the tribal areas; young generation is getting involved in criminal activities. Native youth are not getting proper employment opportunities. They have lost their traditional professions. At present they are not skilled enough to survive in the corporate world. Economic disparities among the tribal people have increased. It has resulted into factionalism on the basis of class structure that has disturbed the harmony of the tribal community.

Concept of Corporate Social Responsibility is a healthy practice of the corporate world towards society at large. Nature and process of CSR depends on the intention of the corporates. Funds in the tribal areas are utilised tactically in such a way that it is less in the interest of natives and more in the interest of corporate houses. They use funds to construct wide roads, schools and health centres. People who live in the tribal areas do not get any priority in these services and it is difficult for them to afford these facilities provided by corporates in the area. District Kinnaur is a glaring example of this phenomenon. Schools, rest-houses and medical facilities are mainly benefitting their employees. Major stakeholders (natives) derive little benefit from them.

On the basis of these findings it is evident that in the era of globalisation and liberalisation, the tribal community is not able to get its due. From the constitutional perspective, the tribes are not able to protect and promote their age old culture along with the process of modernisation. Concept of 'continuity with change' has lost its viability in the present. The policies do not take into consideration the concept of sustainable development and little attention is paid to the indigenous system, evolved in accordance with the local conditions.

Rising disparities between land owners and marginal farmers have also posed a challenge to the ideal of a socialist society which was the dream of the constitution makers for future India.

Suggestions

Government should take into consideration the ecology of the tribal society. Effective decentralised planning system should be evolved on the principle of 'planning according to the local needs and local resources by the local people'. State should not impose anything on them. State, civil society and corporate world should encourage the protection and promotion of their art and culture.

- Tribal community should be trained to adopt new technologies according to their own requirements and ways;
- It should be mandatory to involve the tribes in deciding the development goals;

- Their control over forest land and other natural resources should be protected;
- In the era of Public and Private Partnership (PPP), civil society, NGOs and government should work collectively and take into consideration the diverse views of all the stake holders while deciding the policy framework for the tribals;
- There should be strict riders on the corporate activities keeping in mind the environment and socio-culture milieu of the community;
- To meet the present challenges it is imperative to accord priority to native interests over corporate interests;
- Besides the legislative framework, political leadership should display an inclination to implement the legislative measures to empower the masses;
- Government should plan to bolster the human capabilities as well as infrastructure to meet the flaws of the existing developmental approach, for an inclusive growth;

Notes

Thakur B.R. conducted a primary study in the all the three tribal pockets of Himachal and evaluated the transformation in the area on the bases of the variables: literacy rate, educational patterns, and societal structure (conducted under the aegis of Indian Council of Social Science Research (ICSSR updated in 2012).

Forest Rights Act 2006 is not implemented in the letter and spirit. It is evident during the primary study conducted by Mridula Sharda in 2012 (UGC funded Minor project) and latest developments in 2018 when people of Lippa village agitated on the issue and government's decision to hand over the village land for Keshang power project to the Himachal Pradesh Power Corporation in 2018. People in general and the non-official members of the District Level Committee also endorsed the view that FRA has not been effective in the area after the cabinet decision to hand over the land. People of Kinnaur were also annoyed and they also expressed their resentment and more than 90 per cent people opposed the corporate activities in the area, as per the study of the Inder Negi (2015) (unpublished Ph.D. thesis submitted in Political Science Department HPU).

Bibliography

Agnew, P.D. *Gazetteer of Lahoul and Spiti*, Delhi: Indus Publishing Company, 1899.

Ahluwalia, M.S. *Social, Cultural and Economic History of Himachal Pradesh*, New Delhi: Indian Publishing Company, 1998.

Attri, Rajender. *Himachal Pradesh*, New Delhi: Navrang Publications, 2010.

——, *Himachal Pradesh: A Himalayan Dreamland*, Shimla: Sarla Publications, 2015.

Bahadur, K.P. *Caste, Tribes and Culture of India*, Vol. VI, Haryana, Himachal Pradesh, Punjab, Jammu & Kashmir and Sikkim, New Delhi: Ess Ess Publishers, 1978.

Bajpai, S.C. *Kinnaur in the Himalayans*, New Delhi: Concept Publishing Company, 1981.

——, *Lahaul-Spiti: A Forbidden Land in the Himalaya*, New Delhi: H.G. Publishing Company, 1987.

Balokhra, Jag Mohan. *The Wonderland of Himachal Pradesh*, New Delhi: H.G. Publications, 1985 (2011).

——, *The Paradise: Himachal Pradesh*, New Delhi: H.G. Publications, 2008.

Basu, Ashok Ranjan. *Tribal Development Programmes and Administration in India*, New Delhi: National Book Organization, 1985.

Bhatnagar, S. *Political Theory: An Introduction*, New Delhi: Meenakshi Prakashan, 1984.

Biswas, Ranjan Kumar. *SC, ST and Other Backward Class in India*, New Delhi: Mahaveer and Sons, 2008.

Champion, H.G. and S.K. Seth. *Revised Survey of the Forest Types of India*, New Delhi: Manager of Publications, 1968.

Chandra, Ramesh. *Highlanders of North Western Himalayas,* New Delhi: Inter-India Publications, 1992.

Chaudhary, Minakshi. *Exploring Pangi Himalaya,* New Delhi: Indus Publishing Company, 2002.

Chauhan, Ramesh. *Himachal Pradesh India: A Perspective,* Shimla: Minerva Book House, 1998.

Chhib, S.S. *Kanauras of the Trans-Himalaya,* New Delhi: Ess Ess Publications, 1984.

Das, Hari Har and B.C. Chaudhary. *Political Theory: Traditional and Modern Theory,* New Delhi: National Publishing House, 1999.

Das, S.T. *Tribal Development and Socio-Cultural Matrix,* Delhi: Kanishka Publishers, 1993.

Datta, C.L. *The Raj and the Simla Hill States: Socio-Economic Problems, Agrarian Disturbances and Paramountcy,* New Delhi: ABS Publications, 1984.

Devi, Shakuntla. *Caste System in India,* Jaipur: Pointer Publishers, 1999.

Gill, Manohar Singh. *Himalayan Wonderland: Travels in Lahaul-Spiti,* Delhi: Vikas Publishing House Pvt. Ltd., 1972.

Ghurye, G.S. *The Aborigines, So-called and their Future,* Bombay: Popular Prakashan, 1943.

Harcourt, A.F.P. *The Himalayan District of Kooloo, Lahoul and Spiti,* Delhi: Vivek Publishing House, 1972.

Hasnain, Nadeem. *Tribal India,* New Delhi: Palak Prakashan, 2011.

Huntington, Samuel P. and Jorge I. Dominguez. 'Political Development', in Fred I. Greenstein and Nelson W. Polsby (eds), *Handbook of Political Science, Micro Political Theory,* Vol. 3, Massachusetts: Addison Wesley Pub Co., 1975.

Hutton, J.H. *Caste in India,* Cambridge: Cambridge University Press, 1964.

Inamdar, N.R. *Functioning of Village Panchayat,* New Delhi: Popular Prakashan, 1970.

Indira, R. and Deepak Kumar Behra (ed.), *Gender and Society in India: Rural and Tribal Studies,* Vol. II, New Delhi: Manak Publication, 1999.

Jaseph, Molley. *Women Participation and Development Strategies,* New Delhi: Kanishka Publishers, 1997.

Jerath, Ashok. *The Splendor of Himalaya Art and Culture,* New Delhi: Indus Publishing Company, 1995.

Jharta, Bhawana. *Women and Politics in India,* New Delhi: Deep and Deep Publication, 1998.

Jone, William. *Kinship, Caste, Class and Society,* New Delhi: Cyber Tech. Publications, 2013.

Joseph, Molly. *Women Participation and Development Strategies,* New Delhi: Kanishka Publishing, 1997.

Joshi, Vidyut. *Tribal Situation in India*, New Delhi and Jaipur: Rawat Publications, 1998.

Kapadia, Harish. *Spiti: Adventures in the Terms Himalaya*, New Delhi: Indus Publishing Company, 1996.

Kapur, Suresh. *Scheduled Tribes of Himachal Pradesh*, New Delhi: Navrang Publishers, 1993.

Khan, Yakub Ali. *Tribal Life in India*, Jaipur: RBSA Publishers, 2000.

Khosla, Pran. *From Independence to State Reorganisation*, in Himachal: Past, Present and Future, Shimla: Directorate of Correspondence Courses, 1975.

Kothari, Rajani. *Caste in Indian Politics*, New Delhi: Orient Longman,1970.

Kumar, Anil. *Tribes and Tribal Life*, New Delhi: Sarup and Sons, 1994.

Leach, E.R. (ed.), *Aspects of Caste in India*, Cambridge: Cambridge University Press, 1960.

Majmudar, D.N. *Himalayan Polyandry*, New Delhi: Asia Publishing House, 1962.

Mamgain, M.D. *Himachal Pradesh District Gazetteers: Kinnaur*, Ambala Cant: Quick Printers, 1971.

Mehta, G.S. *Participation of Women in the Panchayati Raj System*, New Delhi: Sarup and Sons, 2002.

Mehta, S.K. and A.R. Chhabra. *Political Theory*, Jalandhar: New Academic Publishing Co., 2005.

Milbrath, Western W. and M.L. Goel. *Political Participation: How and Why Do People get Involved in Politics?*, 2nd ed., Chicago: Rand McNally, 1977.

Mishra, P.C. *Women in India toward Gender Equality*, New Delhi: Author Press, 2006.

Monga, O.P. 'Dynamics of Family Structure among Kinnauras of Himachal Pradesh: Some Reflections', in S.K. Gupta et al., *Tribal Development: Approach and Alternatives*, New Delhi: Indus Publishing Company, 1998.

Mukhi, H.R. *Political Sociology*, New Delhi: SBD Publishers, 1997.

Nanaria, A.L. and T.K. Vaishnavi. 'Tribal Situation in Madhya Pradesh', in Vidyut Joshi (ed.), *Tribal Situation in India*, Jaipur: Rawat Publications, 1998.

Nefrusturna, Galina. *Women in Structures of Political Power*, in Bharati Ray (ed.), *Women and Politics: France, India and Russia*, Calcutta: K.P. Bagchi and Co., 2000.

Negi, T.S. *Scheduled Tribes of Himachal Pradesh*, Meerut: Raj Printers, 1976.

Padovani, Florence (ed.). *Development-Induced Displacement in India and China: A Comparative Look at the Burdens of Growth*, London: Lexington Books, 2016.

Palmer, N.D. *Elections and Political Development: The South Asian Experience*, New Delhi: Vikas Publishing House, 1976.

Panchani, C.S. *The Himalayan Tribes*, Delhi: Konark Publishers, Pvt. Ltd., 1994.

Pant, B.R. *Tribal Demography of India*, New Delhi: Anamika Publishers, 2010.

Pargunan, M. (ed.). 'Women Leadership in Rural Tamil Nadu: Impact of 73rd Constitutional Amendment Act', in *Panchayati Raj System in India*, New Delhi: Kanishka Publishers, 2008.

Parmar, Y.S. *Polyandry in Himalayas*, Delhi: Vikas Publishing House Pvt. Ltd., 1975.

Pati, R.N. and Jagannath Dash. *Tribal and Indigenous People of India*, New Delhi: APH Publishing House, 2002.

Patni, Sushila. *Women Political Elite: Search for Identify*, Jaipur: Printwell, 1994.

Rath, Govinda Chandra. *Tribal Development in India: The Contemporary Debate*, New Delhi: Sage Publications, 2006.

Roy, Kalpana. *Women in India Politics*, New Delhi: Rajat Publication, 1999.

Sah, D.C. and Yatindra Singh (ed). *Tribal Issues in India*, Jaipur: Rawat Publications, 2004.

Sahni, Ram Nath. *Lahaul: The Mystery Land in Himalayas*, New Delhi: Indus Publishing Company, 1994.

Sahu, Chaturbhuj. *Indian Tribal Life*, New Delhi: Sarup and Sons, 2001.

Sanan, Deepak and Dhanu Swadi. *Exploring Kinnaur and Spiti in the Trans-Himalaya*, New Delhi: Indus Publishing Company, 1998.

Sharda, N.K. and T. Raman Sharma. 'Development of Agriculture in Tribal Areas of H.P. Present Scenario and Future Strategies', in S.K. Gupta et al., *Tribal Development, Approach and Alternatives*, New Delhi: Indus Publishing Company, 1998.

Sharda, Mridula. *Evolution of Panchayati Raj in India*, New Delhi: Kanishka Publications, 2010.

Sharma, Arjun. *Caste, Class and Politics in Rural India*, New Delhi: Khanna Publishers, 1993.

Sharma, K.L. *Caste and Class in India*, Jaipur: Rawat Publications, 2010.

Singh, K.S. *Tribal Society in India*, New Delhi: Manohar Publishers, 1985.

——, *The Schedule Tribes*, New Delhi: Oxford University Press,1994.

—— (ed.), *People of India: Himachal Pradesh*, New Delhi: Manohar, 1996.

Singh, Mian Goverdhan. *The History of Himachal Pradesh*, Delhi: Yugbodh Publishing House, 1982.

Singh, Rattan and Alok Kumar. *Panchayati Raj System in India*, New Delhi: Kanishka Publishers and Distributors, 1999.

Singh, S.S. and Suresh Mishra. *Legislative Framework of Panchayati Raj in India*, New Delhi: Intellectual Publishing House, 1993.

Singh, Shailendra. *Caste in India: A Historical Perspective*, New Delhi: Annual Publications Pvt. Ltd., 2007.

Sinha, Ruma Kumar. 'Cultural Change in Tribes of Bihar', in Chaturbhuj Sahu (ed.), *Indian Tribal Life,* New Delhi: Sarup and Sons, 2001.

Srinivasan, Janaki. 'Democracy', in Rajeev Bhargava and Ashok Acharya, *Political Theory: An Introduction,* Delhi: Pearson Longman, 2008.

Srinivas, M.N. *Caste in Modern India and Other Essay,* London: Asia Publishing House,1962.

Thakur, D.S. 'Performance and Strategies for Faster Tribal Development in Himachal Pradesh', in S.K. Gupta et al. (ed.), *Tribal Development: Appraisal and Alternatives,* New Delhi: Indus Publishing Company, 1998.

Thakur, Devendra and D.N. Thakur. *Role of Voluntary Organization in Tribal Development* (Tribal Life in India–10), New Delhi: Deep and Deep Publication, 1997.

Thakur, Devendra. *Socio-Economic Development of Tribes in India,* New Delhi: Deep and Deep Publications, 1986.

Tobdan. *History and Religions of Lahaul,* New Delhi: Book Today, 1984.

Verba, Sidney V. and Norman H. Nie. *Participation in America: Political Democracy and Social Equality,* New York: Harper and Row Publishers, 1972.

Verma, V.B. *Gujars: A Nomadic Tribe in Himachal Pradesh,* Delhi: B.R. Publishing Corporation, 1999.

Verma, V. *Gaddis of Dhauladhar: A Transhipment Tribe of the Himalayas,* New Delhi: Indus Publishing Company, 1996.

——. *Pangi: A Tribal Habitat in Mid-Himalaya,* New Delhi: Indus Publishing Company, 1996.

——. *Spiti: A Buddhist Land in Western Himalaya,* Delhi: B.R. Publishing Corporation, 1997.

Widow, Father and Nicholas J. Smith. *Global Social Justice,* NY: Routledge , 2011.

Articles in Journals

Biswas, Sudipta. 'Implementation of PESA: Issues, Challenges and Way Forward', in *International Research Journal of Social Sciences,* Vol. 4(12), 49–54 December 2015.

Biswa, S.K. 'Devolution of Power and Utilization of Resources, under Panchayati Raj System in Andaman and Nicobar Island', *Journal of Public Administration,* Vol. LVI, January–March 2010.

Connell, R.W. 'The State, Gender and Sexual Politics', *Theory and Society,* Vol. 19, 1990.

Dhaka, Rajvir S. and Sunita Dhaka. 'Women in Grassroots Democracy in Haryana: A Case Study of SC Women', *Kurukshetra,* Vol. 52, No. 5, March 2004.

Hauser, Ciatter. 'Changing Images of Caste and Politics', *Seminar* No. 450, February 1997: 48.

Hazra, Anupam. 'Migration: Still a Survival Strategy for Rural India', *Kurukshetra,* Vol. 59, November 2010.

Khanna, Manuka. 'Political Participation of Women in India', *Indian Journal of Political Science,* Vol. 70, No. 1, January–March, 2009.

Narayan, D. 'Local Government without Capacity building ten years of Panchayati Raj', *Economic and Political Weekly,* Vol. XL, No. 26, June, 2005.

Narayanan, Pradeep. 'Empowerment through Participation How Effective in this Approach', *Economic and Political Weekly,* Vol. XL, No. 30, June, 2003.

Nayak, Ramesh C. 'Panchayati Raj in Haryana Experience', *Kurukshetra,* Vol. 52, No. 5, March 2004.

Nilofer, S. Waseem Ahmad and Pattranzala, Parveen. 'Women's Political Participation and Changing Pattern of Leadership in Rural Area U.P.', *The Indian Journal of Political Science,* Vol. XLIX, No. 3, July–September 2008.

Sahoo, Sarbeswar. 'The Politics of Tribal Resisenance in Orissa', *Indian Journal of Political Science,* Vol. 68, No. 2, April–June, 2007.

Schonfeld, William R. 'The Meaning of Democratic Participation', *World Politics,* Vol. XXVIII, No. 1, 1975.

Sethi, Renu. 'Determinant of Women Active Political Participation', *The Indian Journal of Political Science,* Vol. 49, No. 4, October–December, 1988.

Singh, Jhanshi. 'Tribal Women in Local Governance: A Case Study', *The Indian Journal of Political Science,* Vol. LXXVI, No. 3, July–September 2015.

Sisodia, Yatindra Singh. 'Peoples Participation in Gram Sabha: A Case Study of Rural Madhya Pradesh', *Kurukshetra,* Vol. 54, No. 7, May 2006.

Subrahmanyam, K. Siva. 'Empowerment of Women and Marginalized Groups in Panchayats', *Kurukshetra,* Vol. 50, No. 7, May 2002.

Thakur, Gayak, Ram. 'Women Participation in Gram Sabha with Special Reference to Himachal Pradesh', *Vidhan Mala,* Vol. II, No. 11, December 2008.

Vyas, Girija. 'Women Empowerment: Remedy for Social Elevation', *Yojana,* Vol. 52, September 2008.

Vyasa, Purnima and Vayasula, Vinod. 'Women in Panchayati Raj Grassroots, Democracy in Malgudi', *Economic and Political Weekly,* Vol. XXXIV, No. 52, 25 December 1999.

Acts and Bills

Government of India: 73rd Amendment Act.

Government of Himachal Pradesh: Part C State Act, 1951.

Government of Himachal Pradesh: Panchayati Raj Act, 1968.

Government of Himachal Pradesh: Panchayati Raj Act, 1994.

Government of India: PESA Act, 1996.

Government of Himachal Pradesh: Panchayati Raj, General Rule, 1997.

Government of India: Forest Rights Act, 2006.

Reports

Annual Administrative Report 2010–11, Himachal Pradesh Panchayati Raj Department.

Annual Administrative Report Government of India (2013–14).

Annual Report (2012–13), Ministry of Tribal Affairs, Government of India.

Ashok Mehta Committee Report.

Balwant Rai Mehta Committee Report.

Census of India, 2001.

Census of India, 2011.

Cohen, John M. & Norman T. Uphoff. *Participation's Place in Rural Development: Seeking Clarity Through Specificity*, World Development, Elsevier. 1980, Vol. 8 (3).

Brief Fact of Himachal Pradesh (1997) Shimla: Economic and Statistic Department Himachal Pradesh.

Brief Fact of Himachal Pradesh (2006) Shimla: Economic and Statistic Department Himachal Pradesh.

Daleep Singh Bhuria Committee Report.

District Census (2011) Kinnaur: Handbook.

Economic Survey of Himachal Pradesh (2013–14) Shimla: Economic and Statistics Department Himachal Pradesh.

Economic Survey of Himachal Pradesh (2014–15) Shimla: Economic and Statistics Department Himachal Pradesh.

G.V.K. Rao Committee Report.

Hanumantha Rao Committee Report.

Human Development Report, United National Developmental Programmes.

L.M. Singhvi Committee Report.

Rural Development and Panchayati Raj Department, Himachal Pradesh, 2000.

Statistical Report of Scheduled Tribe Profile 2013(GOI).

World Bank Development Report 2015.

Encyclopedia

International Encyclopedia of Social Sciences, Vol. 12. New York: Macmillan, 1968.

The New Encyclopedia, Britannica, Inc. William Benton, Publishers, Vol. 14, 1993.

Websites and Dictionaries

Collins Dictionary, 1987.

Goodwin, Robert E. (ed.). *The Oxford Handbook of Contextual Political Analysis*, NY: Oxford Press, 1996.

Oxford Dictionary, 1993.

Webster's Dictionary, 1996.

www.himachalpanchayatirajdeptt

www.hp.gov.nic.in

www.ministryoftribalaffairs

Unpublished Works

Sharda, Mridula. *Grassroots Politics and Panchayati Raj in Himachal Pradesh: Before and After Seventy Third Amendment*, A Thesis Submitted to the Himachal Pradesh University, Shimla, for the Degree of Doctor of Philosophy in Department of Political Science, 2001.

Sharda, Mridula. *Effectiveness of the Marginalized Sections in Tribal Communities: A Case Study of Kinner Community in Himachal Pradesh*, Project Report Submitted to UGC, 2013.

Devi, Lata. *Women Participation in Panchayati Raj Institutions: A Case Study of Karsog Block*, A Thesis Submitted to the Himachal Pradesh University, Shimla for the Degree of Doctor of Philosophy in Department of Political Science, 2012.

Newspapers

Amar Ujala

Divya Himachal

The Hindu

The Times of India

The Tribune

Index